A Harvest Yet To Reap
A History of Prairie Women

A Harvest Yet To Reap

A History of Prairie Women

Researched and Compiled by

Linda Rasmussen
Lorna Rasmussen
Candace Savage
Anne Wheeler

Introductory Essays by

Candace Savage

The Women's Press
Toronto, Canada

Canadian Cataloguing in Publication Data

Main entry under title:

A Harvest yet to reap

Bibliography: p.
Includes index.
ISBN 0-88961-030-4 bd. ISBN 0-88961-029-0 pa.

1. Women—Prairie Provinces—History
2. Women—Prairie Provinces—Biography
3. Frontier and pioneer life—Prairie Provinces.
I. Rasmussen, Linda, 1950-

FC3237.H37   301.41'2'09712   C76-015025-7
F1060.9.H

Edited by Christa Van Daele
Cover Design by Donna Bobier and Elizabeth Martin
Typeset at Women's Press, Toronto, Ontario, in co-operation with Dumont Press Graphix, Kitchener, Ontario
Printed and Bound at the John Deyell Company, Willowdale, Ontario
Lithographed by union labour at the John Deyell Company, Lindsay, Ontario

I grew indignant as I read the history and saw how little the people ever counted, and longed for the time when I would be old enough to say something....

When I wrote I would write of the people who do the work of the world and I would write it from their side of the fence.

—*Nellie McClung*
Clearing In The West

ACKNOWLEDGEMENTS

This book would not have been possible without the financial assistance of Mrs. Margaret H. Brine, whose generous contribution allowed us to begin the research. We are also indebted to the Women's Programme of the Secretary of State for their financial support.

We wish to thank George Melnyk for his encouragement and support, Magpie Media for sharing their files, Cheryl Malmo for additional research, Arthur Savage for his interest and advice, Frieda Koplowicz for patiently typing and retyping our material, and the many women who gave us interviews and photographs. We extend our thanks, finally, to the librarians of the following archives: the Public Archives of Canada, the Provincial Archives of Manitoba, the Provincial Archives of Alberta, and the Saskatchewan Archives. Their advice and assistance facilitated the task of our research enormously.

Contents

Preface

This book began with different women in different places at different times, all with a common problem: where to start? If you want to study the history of women on the Canadian prairies, how do you know what to look at first? With no established chronologies of significant events on which to rely, how do you tell which issues and sources are most important? Can you ever hope to weave a collective history from the tangle of individual women's experiences? That is what this book tries to do. It is an overview of the history of white women on the Canadian prairies in the early years of agricultural settlement; it is a place to begin.

The idea of assembling the material in the way you find it here grew out of a practical difficulty. Two of our number, Anne Wheeler and Lorna Rasmussen, put several years work into *Great Grand Mother*, their half-hour film on pioneer women. By the time they were finished, they had collected a large cardboard box of unfiled documents, a stack of filmed interviews, and a sprawling pile of photographs. There, all jumbled together in the post-production confusion, were diaries, letters, reminiscences—images and accounts of the lives of prairie women. How much of the information had gone into the film? a tenth? a twentieth? It was dispiriting to think that all the rest would once again be lost in personal memories and crumbling newsprint.

These same feelings were shared by Candace Savage, a writer who had been collecting similar research for a series of articles, and the Magpie Media group who had produced a slide-tape presentation on women's property rights prior to 1917. We all agreed that a book could begin to bring the pieces together, making them accessible to a wider audience.

We knew that our information was incomplete: it was as if some of the jigsaw pieces had been lost or hidden. We didn't know how many were missing or where they would fit. All we had was a box of fragments, and from them we were to guess what the finished picture could be. This book is our guess.

The outline we came up with is very simple: most women came to the West in the early 1900's as farm homemakers *(Prelude: Moving West)*. During the first perilous years on the land, they and everyone else who could work were preoccupied with trying to stay alive long enough to get a farm established *(Life on the Prairies)*. Kept apart by distance and overwork, women didn't have much time to visit each other, but they had plenty of time to think about their experiences and about their legal and social status *(Rethinking the Role)*. As economic conditions became more secure and settlement more dense, they began to get together, at first for company and advice, and later for community improvement and political reform *(Organizing for Reform)*. They placed particular emphasis on laws which affected the home *(Changing the Law)*. This work, which flowered most dramatically in the women's suffrage campaign *(Winning the Vote)* grew sturdily out of the experiences and needs of prairie women. Then, just when it should have been time to reap the results, the movement withered like a frozen crop, leaving its leaders to wonder what had gone wrong *(Epilogue)*.

While this scenario was useful to us in organizing the book, we recognize that it is an oversimplification. Women did not arrive *en masse* at the beginning of the settlement period as our outline implies; they arrived in surges as early as 1812 and as late as 1920. Not all of them lived on farms or joined women's organizations. Rather than tailor the facts to fit our scheme, we have resigned ourselves to some untidyness. For example, if a woman came to the prairies at the "wrong" time, we've still included her story in the *Prelude*. Wherever possible, we have given precedence to a chronology of psychological, social, and political development rather than to a simple chronology of dates.

To prevent you from getting lost, we've included introductory notes which explain our reasons for grouping the excerpts the way we have, and to indicate ways in which the material may be biased by our interests and our sources. The documents we've included in the book are a fair reflection of what is available in libraries and archives. There are the writings and papers of a few influential, middle class women like Nellie McClung, Violet McNaughton and Emily Murphy. There are the records of a number of women's organizations, and government documents relating to legal reforms. The historical record is biased in favour of public personages and their political activities, and this book mirrors that bias.

Material on the everyday life of "ordinary" women is relatively difficult to come by. Even histories of individual families or communities, many of them written by women, generally leave centre stage clear for Hubby or Dad. Women have seldom felt themselves to be makers of history. For generations they've been stagehands and understudies, doing much of the work while someone up front took all the bows. Few women have thought their lives important or interesting enough to merit documentation, and no one has ever given them much argument on the point.

What you find in this book has been gleaned mainly from reminiscences, letters and newspapers, all of them in

English. Aside from a few interviews, which we were fortunate enough to conduct ourselves, we have very little material from non-white, non-English-speaking communities. This is a serious deficiency in the book, which once again reflects the deficiencies of archive collections. Documents in languages other than English are rare and seldom translated.

If the four of us who worked on the book have sometimes felt unequal to the task we set for ourselves, we have been inspired and sustained by the women whom we discovered. All of us grew up in the '50's, when the usual models of womanhood were Mom and Debbie Reynolds singing about "French Heeled Shoes". We were excited to find heroines we could call our own—magnificent women of whom we'd never before heard a word. How did it happen, we wondered, that their lives had been so completely forgotten? Why were we painfully rediscovering things which they'd seen clearly sixty years before? We approached them at first with curiosity, expecting to find them dated and quaint. We view them now with admiration and respect.

Obviously, ours was not the first generation to be humiliated by women's traditional role; ours was not the first generation of women to dare to question. We began to realize how powerful our image of the past had been in limiting our sense of our own possibilities. There is strength in the knowledge that among our foremothers were women who confronted their pain and frustration with sincerity and intelligence, just as we try to meet our own. As prairie women, we are part of a tradition, rooted in the past.

The history of prairie women is there for us to reap. Perhaps this book will make it a little easier...

I Prelude: Moving West

The history of women on the Canadian prairies extends back tens of thousands of years to the first nomadic band which wandered out onto the plains. The oldest written records of their experiences date from less than three hundred years ago when the fur traders moved west from Hudson's Bay and the St. Lawrence valley to set up shop along the major inland waterways. As most history books tell it, the fur trade was an all-male enterprise, but on closer inspection, we find the familiar pattern of "the woman behind the man".

For the most part, the traders left their European wives and sweethearts at home in Great Britain or Quebec. Out in the fur country, it made a lot more sense to depend on local labour—Indian women who could not only cook, sew and bear babies, but who knew a poisonous plant or grub-infested cariboo when they saw one. Spinning wheels and crocks of canned chicken were fine in their place, but at Fort Churchill or Cumberland House, it was a lot handier to know someone who could make snowshoes and catch fish. If she could also dress furs and speak the local language, she was a decided business asset. No need to pay her, of course, and should you leave the country or simply feel bored, you could abandon her and children without a backward glance.

Not all fur trade marriages followed that course. When David Thompson retired to Scotland, his Métis wife Charlotte went with him. According to one account, she also accompanied him through the Rockies to the mouth of the Columbia River, a journey which made *him* famous. Presumably, Charlotte didn't just go along for the fresh air and exercise. Typically enough for those pre-pill days, she was pregnant: within a month of their return to Rocky Mountain House, she had a baby.

Considering the pitiless demands made on fur trade women, the first European woman known to have visited the prairies was wise to come disguised as a man. In the early 1800's, Mary Fubbester (better known to history as 'the Orkney Lass') signed on as a Hudson's Bay Company clerk in order to pursue a lover who had run off to Canada. According to one of her colleagues, she worked "at anything and well like the rest of the men". But when she gave away her secret by having a baby, she was immediately shipped back home in disgrace.

Like Mary, the first white woman to settle permanently on the prairies came to follow her man. Marie-Anne Lagimodière had been married only a few weeks when her ex-voyageur husband announced his intention to return to the fur trade. He could scarcely have expected her to come along. What use could she possibly be, this priest's house-keeper from small-town French Canada? Whatever his doubts and her fears, Marie-Anne went along and survived, but according to her biographer, life was grim. One day, for example, she rode through a buffalo stampede with a baby under one arm. As she held on desperately with her free hand, her pony galloped, stumbled and turned, chasing now one, now another of the snorting herd. Back in camp that evening, she gave birth to her second child, a son, who was named Laprairie to commemorate the wild ride. As if she would have ever forgotten!

Of course, the fur trade wasn't the only frontier institution which looked to women for support. Officers of the North West Mounted police brought their wives out West. Protestant missionaries on the prairies depended upon female lay workers and women in their own families to teach in the mission schools. The Roman Catholic nuns were in a class by themselves. The Sisters were among the most independent and self-reliant of the early women settlers. Perhaps this was because the convents attracted a strong-willed and resolute breed. For centuries, holy orders had been one of the few avenues open to women with ambitions in community service or the professions. The first nuns in the West, four Sisters of Charity from Montreal, arrived at St. Boniface in the summer of 1844. There they fulfilled the combined roles of catechist, social worker, pharmacist, nurse and doctor. Their first project was to organize a travelling medical practice and a hospital. Similar services were provided elsewhere in the "wild" west, first by the Grey Nuns, and later by other nursing and teaching orders. Missionary women established many of the basic institutions which made agricultural settlement feasible.

While the missionaries helped make settlement possible, the westward push of the American frontier made it increasingly necessary. In 1860, the Hudson's Bay Company stood by helplessly while its territory in Oregon was engulfed by the United States. At that time, American politicians and railway contractors were making no secret of their longing to control the Canadian North West as well. Naturally, Canadian and British interests were alarmed by this prospect. Anyone could see that the westward expansion of agriculture had made American industry boom: it was conceivable that settlement could do the same for Canadians, providing they could stake their claim to the prairies first.

By 1885, the Canadian government finally had all the machinery for western settlement. A protective tariff was created to keep out inexpensive goods from south of the border, leaving the field clear for higher priced Canadian products. The CPR had built a national railway in return for receiving hundreds of sections of first-class prairie land and guarantees of monopoly. A land policy offered a free quarter-section to all comers (as long as the comers were male, that is). All that was lacking were settlers.

During the 1870's and 80's, immigrants trickled into

the West from eastern Canada, Europe and the United States. But it was not until 1896, when Clifford Sifton became Minister of the Interior, that the long-awaited surge of western migration really began. Sifton's department, in company with the CPR, hawked the West throughout North America and Europe. The officials didn't have much to say about high prices or freight rates, but they could be very convincing when the conversation turned to easy prosperity and free land. If one were to believe Sifton's salespeople, the prairies offered thousands of square miles of sun-warmed prosperity and opportunity, not only for the settlers, but also for their children.

They came from eastern Canada, Great Britain and the United States, although significant numbers arrived from Austria-Hungary, Scandinavia and eastern Europe as well. The married women probably came for the same reasons which brought their men: religious persecution, political oppression, thin stony farmland, factory-town grime. Stirred by the vision, they came with enthusiasm and hope. Others came reluctantly, following their husbands' initiative.

For independent, single women, there were more positive inducements. Rumour had it that the prairies were a paradise for women who sought financial self-sufficiency. It was said that jobs were plentiful, wages high and society tolerant of female wage-earners. Although few women were eligible for free homesteads, it was believed that those with money and experience could buy land and run a farm of their own. Especially in the British press, emigration to the prairies was often touted as an alternative to careful penury and to marriage.

Immigration officials were quick to temper these reports. Yes, there was work for women, they agreed, but as maids, and as maids only. What the prairies really offered to unmarried women, the propagandists hinted, was thousands of single men. Of the 900,000 people who moved West between 1900 and 1911 (the period of greatest immigration), almost two-thirds were men. By the end of the decade, unmarried men between the ages of 20 and 24 outnumbered eligible women by 2 to 1 in Manitoba and by 4 to 1 in Saskatchewan and Alberta. For the 25 to 34 age group, the ratios were 3 to 1 in Manitoba and 8 to 1 further west!

Both the bachelors and the immigration officials agreed that a person couldn't establish a family farm without a farm family to help with the work. And families meant women. The propaganda machine put a good deal of effort into attracting the right sort of single woman: strong, accustomed to house-work, and interested in marriage. If she were cultured and English-speaking, the sort who would rear good British subjects and "raise the tone" of the community, so much the better. If not, any sturdy, skilled worker would do.

Women were welcome to come as wives, poor wives hoping to be rich wives, servants working for wives, daughters certain to become wives. They were to bear and educate children, work on the homesteads, and make the men comfortable so that they would stay. But what were they to get in return? The immigration literature invited women to anticipate a leisurely and refined domesticity, untroubled by worry or fatigue. It was one of the promises which the prairie was not prepared to deliver.

"Do you know" remarked W.D. Scott, to a Toronto newspaper reporter, "one of the greatest needs in the North West at the present time? It is women, simply women. Married men with their wives are contented enough out there, but single men on farms are apt to get lonely. If girls could only be persuaded to go out there they would be sure of good situations, and I tell you it would not be long before they would get married."

—MacLeod Gazette
May 15, 1896

Emigrants for Canada on an Atlantic liner

BUY FARMS IN ALBERTA! Leave home after Easter, sow grain, take in the golden harvest and come home with pockets full of money in time for Thanksgiving dinner!

—Old Days And Old Timers

The women wanted in Western Canada are those healthy, countrybred women who love and understand animal life, and who prefer the freedom of the country to the conventionalities of the town. They must be women of some culture, but who have had training in domestic arts by practising them, and who will keep up the tone of the men with whom they mix by music and book-lore when the day's work is over.

—The Canadian Gazette
January 30, 1902

"The best crop and pasture land in the world"
—*CPR propaganda in Dutch*

The farm housewife is a busy woman; she is also capable. In the morning, busy at her churn making butter, picking and packing eggs, pruning fruit bushes, weeding the garden, feeding or "dressing" poultry for market, cultivating flowers, getting meals and keeping house. In the afternoon, you may meet the same lady dressed in a city model gown, driving her horse towards town, her carriage piled high with fruits from farm acres, and if you follow her to shop in the market place you will discover her shrewdly bartering her wares for manufactured necessities. The same pair of hands, busy in the morning with the butter pat, may in the afternoon guide the embroidery needle, or with the palette and brush reproduce a local bit of color.

—Home Life Of Women In Western Canada
C.P.R. propaganda booklet, 1907

Canada ....is a country where a young woman who possesses practical skill in domestic science—held to be the first and finest of all accomplishments—is looked upon with consideration and respect. Canadians have a due appreciation of such services and are prepared to pay well for them.

While we require twenty to thirty thousand men to assist in reaping our bountiful harvest annually, there are but few young women come to the assistance of the ladies, whose duty it is to provide for their household and for the additional help. A great number of very worthy girls have come to this country from time to time, it is true, but on account of the excellent opportunities there are out here for them to settle in life in homes of their own, household help appears to be getting steadily scarcer as times goes on.

—To The Young Women Of England, Ireland And Scotland
C.P.R. propaganda booklet

*Propaganda
for prosperous
West,*
circa *1916*

Farmers, Farm Laborers and Female Domestic servants are the only people whom the Canadian Immigration Dept. advise to emigrate to Canada.

Canada offers many opportunities of employment and advancement to the right type of woman. Women trained in housework or willing to take such training can be assured of good wages, steady employment and reasonable employers. The demand in both city and country and in all the provinces is very great, and any woman wishing to come to Canada is strongly urged to consider this branch of employment.

The houseworker most in demand is the trained cook general. Many hotels in cities and towns are applying for chamber-maids. Hospitals, schools and other institutions need women as cooks, kitchen helps, dining-room and ward maids. In a number of cities there is a demand for trained dayworkers, women who can give two or three hours daily or sometimes the full day and live out. This work is mostly in demand in apartment houses and small families. One woman can thus serve several families.

The status and social opportunities which are afforded to houseworkers in Canada are a great inducement to women of ambition. Liberal and even generous wages are offered to all who can give acceptable service.

—Women Wanted In Canada
Propaganda booklet

A young man without experience should be well content with board only for the first month or more while learning—then he may get $20-$40, even $50 per month. High wages are paid domestic servants—in town $10 to $15 per month, on ranches $12 to $18—also marriage prospects are good.

—What Is Paid Helpers On Alberta Farms And Ranches
Government pamphlet

All women unaccompanied by husband, father, or mother, coming to Canada to engage in housework or industrial employment, must receive an emigration permit and travel in a conducted party.

—Regulation Of The Canadian Department Of Immigration

Domestics landing in Canada, circa *1911*

When I speak of quality, I have in mind something that is quite different from what is in the mind of the average writer or speaker upon the question of immigration. I think that a stalwart peasant in the sheep-skin coat, born on the soil whose forefathers had been farmers for generations, with a stout wife and half-a-dozen children is good quality.

> —*Clifford Sifton*
> Minister of the Interior
> Speech to the Toronto Board of Trade, 1922

Much has been said about the kind of immigrants we should encourage. Sir Clifford Sifton is quoted as saying that "What he considered to be quality in immigration was a sturdy peasant in sheepskin coat with a big wife and four or five children." If the picture which Sir Clifford's words bring to my mind is correct, then what is aimed at is a peasant class of farmer who will work long hours, whose wife and children will likewise work long hours, and who will be content with a very low standard of living. If that is the only solution for western agriculture then the prospect is not very bright for the men and women already on the land, for sooner or later they too must get down to the standard of peasantry or quit.

> —*Violet McNaughton*
> The Torch
> *May, 1923*

Miss
Barbara
Wylie

BARBARA WYLIE TO ORGANIZE BOYCOTT OF THE DOMINION

London, June 3—
"Until Canada has done justice to its own women", she says, "we will urge the women of England not to go there. We are told that Canada is a woman's paradise. It is nothing of the kind. A woman's life in Canada is extremely hard, and lonely, and it is because of their loneliness that the asylums there are being filled with women, who are driven mad by the loneliness. They are caged in a 'shack' often miles from any populated district. Turn your back on Canada."

> —Moose Jaw Evening Times
> *June 18, 1913*

Immigrants Moving West circa 1911

SALVATION ARMY IS TAKING UP WAR WIDOWS' SCHEME IN EARNEST

The commissioners are doing a prospective tour of the Dominion in the interests of a War Widow scheme which General Booth has inaugurated, out of sympathy for the vast number who are deprived of husbands and fathers as a result of the present terrible conflict.

The humaneness of this scheme will readily be seen when one considers that the census returns of the United Kingdom previous to the war shows a preponderance of females over males by nearly a million and a half, and the war will considerably increase this number.

...any plan for the consolidation of the Empire which overlooks the necessity for attempting to secure a more equal distribution of the sexes will have failed in one of the most essential details.

—The Edmonton Journal
March 7, 1916

A great many young married women, the British brides of Canadian soldiers, came to Canada by ship in 1919. Their husbands were to follow at an early date. The girls mixed freely with the other passengers, and talked much of "the Land of Promise" to which they were coming. They had high hopes, and some very amusing ideas of what their new life would be like....They have left a land which is home, to come to a strange land, although in time it may become very dear to them. Their friends are all over yonder; no understanding old friends here to turn to for companionship. In many instances their husbands are almost strangers to them; it was an intermittent wartime acquaintanceship, and they have yet to learn what their husbands are like.

—Nor-West Farmer
April 21, 1919

Families landing in Canada

MARRIAGE AGENCIES

A new matrimonial agency is being extensively advertised throughout Western Canada by a London, England firm, which evidently thinks that the bachelors of the West are in a deplorable state and anxious one and all to wed....doubtless there are less favored spots than Pincher Creek in the great North-West, and the obliging offer of the firm to provide a wife for five dollars down and forty-five on thirty days after the safe performance of the marriage ceremony will probably meet many takers.

The advertisement is nicely worded. For instance it described the terrible fate to which thousands of "good, intelligent and attractive girls" are destined in England, nothing but the prospect of "living and dying as old maids", surely a horrible destiny. Will not the youth and chivalry of Western Canada at once rise up and rescue these damsels from such fate?...The applicant besides his five dollars must send such particulars of himself as "a sensible girl would expect" and here is where the hardships will come in. For if the application had not to be accompanied by references from a clergyman or the police, all would be left to the honesty of the man himself.

—The Rocky Mountain Echo
Pincher Creek, Alberta
August 2, 1904

Everybody waited for the train or stage coach to arrive to see if there were any unmarried girls coming to town. The old-timers at Macleod tell me that the arrival of the stage was the big moment for every bachelor in town.

Some of the more ardent bachelors would climb up to the tops of houses and watch with field-glasses, to see if the stage was approaching. As it drew nearer, they could look inside and study the prospects. When at last it drew up in front of the hotel, there would be a regular stag-line of awkward, sun-tanned men, every one of them wondering whether his fate, his destiny, his future might not be stepping down onto the wooden sidewalk...

In one case the bridegroom-to-be was a Mountie officer who went to great trouble to avoid being disappointed.

His bride was due in on the train. But he wasn't going to meet the train...no! He stationed himself on a hillside near the station armed with a powerful pair of binoculars. At last the train came in, and the bride-elect stepped down. Finding no one there to meet her, she walked up and down the platform.

Meanwhile, the Mountie had his binoculars trained upon her and was giving the lady a careful and thorough-going study. At last, he came to the decision that she wouldn't do. He dispatched his orderly with a note of regret and sufficient funds to send the woman back to her home.

—*"Laughter In The West"*
Old Days and Old Timers

Bachelor camp

One morning, after reading the paper,...a man who had recently emigrated from Ireland to Eastern Canada announced to his wife: "Mary Jane, there are a lot of people going west next month. *We* are going *with* them. Begin getting your things together. I'll put the house up for rent right away." Mary Jane gazed speechlessly at her husband. It had been hard enough to leave dear old Ireland. And now, to face another unknown land, before she was even settled in this new one! She couldn't do it!

Yet, she knew she would do it. James had spoken. His word was law. Indeed, it had been that way when she married him. She had never intended to marry him. But James had said "We're getting married in the morning, Coleen, and we're taking that fine big boat for the big new land, Canada, in the afternoon. So pack your things tonight, Coleen. I'll be around early in the morning. Yes, I've got the passages, here in my pocket." Then he had kissed her and disappeared before she could find speech. It had all happened just like that. And now it was happening again! Seeing the distressed look on her face, he wrapped his strong arms around her, tilted her face so that he could look into her eyes, and asked, in a voice as gentle and sweet as dripping honey, "You wouldn't let me go away out there all alone, now, would you? And you wouldn't want to be staying here all alone, either, would you, with no one to protect you? No, my little Coleen, we stay together, and in that great, new land we'll grow wealthy one day. Then I'll take you back to Ireland, like a Princess. You'll have everything you've ever wanted to have."

—*L.V. Belvadere Arnette*
"Profile of James Patrick"
Pioneer Prairie Profiles

A gently reared girl from Glasgow came out to marry a young man she had not seen for several years. Instead of spending some time at Montreal, as had been arranged, she changed her plans and came straight west, sending a wire in the expectations that it would be delivered promptly as in Scotland. The telegram lay in the post office waiting for the young man....When the prospective bride arrived and found no one to meet her, she went to an hotel and succumbed to hysterics. However she knew... [which clergyman] was to have married them, so she found her way to the Manse. Inquiry revealed that the telegram was still lying in the post office, so a message was sent to the young man. He came in a wagon to take out the luggage. He wore overalls and was covered with mud, and perhaps needed a shave—a far different sight from the well-groomed lad she remembered. His only thought was to rush to see her...without tidying up, and when she saw him she fainted.

Later he persuaded her to visit the farm he had been setting in order for her coming. Going out, she was thrown out of the wagon on a rough stretch of road. She decided she could not marry him and live in this strange country. However she went to visit friends at Red Deer, and after the bridegroom came to see her again dressed as she remembered him, she realized this new country had new ways, she decided she would marry him—which she did, and an excellent wife she made.

Honeymoon couple on the Edson-Grand Prairie Trail, 1914

I sympathize with immigrants when they arrive in this country at first for a more disappointed man than I was, I think, never landed at Winnipeg. Had not been for the pluck of my good wife I believe I never would have taken my trunks from the station. I would have taken our tickets right back to Glasgow. How thankful I have been that I had a wife who had such pluck. To her I give the credit to this day, for both my success and also that of my sons.

—*William Gibson*
Farms and Farmers in Western Canada
Propaganda booklet, 1904

Taking eight children between the ages of four and sixteen, with an outfit such as ours, was an undertaking which required courage. We left Calgary in high spirits under the direction of an Indian guide. Alberta's traditionally clear sunny weather was smiling upon us. Fifteen miles per day was our average speed. The youngsters and I usually kept ahead of the wagons. We picked berries and flowers while on this greatest lark of our lives.

—*Mrs. Margaret M. Lawrence*
Across Canada's Pioneer Trails

Starting for the homestead, 1913

O, the prairie. I cannot describe to you our *first impressions*. Its vastness, dreariness, loneliness is appalling...the last 15 hours travelling have been like the sea on a very smooth day, without beginning or end.

> —*Mary Georgina Hall*
> A Lady's Life On A Farm In Manitoba

Can you imagine being able to hear silence? I have stood outside alone and listened—absolute quiet prevailed. It filled the air. It must have been like the garden of Eden, I think.

> —Life On The Prairie

I left that gay city of Chicago to start life anew on these broad prairies of Saskatchewan....Oh my friend when one leaves the bright lights, the theatres, the beautiful parks, the wonderful shopping places, and last but not least the wonderful churches, with their good choirs, grand pipe organs, and famous minister of the Gospel, all to settle down on a farm out where the coyotes yell and the jack rabbits run, and the caw of the crows can be heard, you must surely know there is some contrast. But the one thing here and the big thing too, that help to make up for the beautiful things left behind are those glorious sunsets, which light up the sky and all earth with those infinite hues that can be seen in no comparable place out of the northern countries.

> —Saskatchewan Homesteading Experiences

In this our...first year naturally we had not been able to get a crop in, coming too late, but we...had been busy all summer preparing it for the spring of 1904; breaking and cultivating this virgin land. The task was not an easy one for city born people but we loved this country, the freedom of it all—the wide open spaces, and the love of adventure was in our blood. This, with a determination to make good whatever the hardships, was all the incentive we required to make a success of farming. We all had the will to work and work we did—with all our hearts, and mind, and soul. None of us knew anything about farming when we first came here, but we soon learned.

When I think of the silly pink teas in the cities, how small a way it does seem to spend one's time, after working in the great open air in large wide spaces, tilling the sod under wonderful blue skies and making a home out of barren virgin land.

> —*Lucie Johnson*
> Against The Wind

Homesteading near Lloydminster

She strained her eyes for a glimpse of her new home around the hills and saw what she felt certain must be the site and "there's the stable", she said. When she really got there it was not a stable but the house instead, her first Saskatchewan home.

—*Mrs. Pauline Denny*
Early History Of Swift Current

When Mrs. McNeil saw the sod house which was to be her home, all dreams of a cozy comfortable little cabin were shattered and she sat down and cried.

—*Mary C. Bailey*
Reminiscences Of Pioneer Life, 1908

It was a none too large rectangular box placed right in the middle of the world that my newly acquired husband dumped me into at the end of our fifty mile jaunt.

He called it a shack. This I resented, and although the entire building was no longer than the dining room of my old Ontario home it was to be my home and I called it a house.

My heart almost stopped still however when I stepped inside. However was I going to make that one fourteen by sixteen room, into a kitchen, bedroom and sitting room. I did it though and have had as many as eight visitors at one time.

—Life on the Prairie

Tarpaper shack

The roof in most of those log houses was of sod, better fitted to preserve heat than to keep out moisture. Ours ...was no exception. In June we had a spell of very rainy weather and there were few dry spots to be found in the house. Papa spread canvas across poles above the beds to keep them dry. I remember Edie holding an umbrella over Mama while she crouched before the fireplace frying sour-dough pancakes for the family. It was too wet to attempt baking bread outside. Willie sat under the table watching, while May and I retreated to our bed to eat in comfort. A day or so after the rain ceased, but the roof still dripped from its water-laden sods.

—Account Of Pioneer Life

The "turf house" was a sort of remnant of the old cave dwellers. It was dug right out of the hill and the owners said was always warm, even in "40 below" weather. There was a father and mother and three little children and a young baby. The mother was the most unhappy depressed woman I ever saw. She told me how she hated the country and had never wanted to come, "My mother said it would kill me and I know it will" she said. She made me feel quite sad. I gave her some little books I had but did not feel able to talk to her as I would like.

...The woman we were to visit was the sister-in-law of the poor little woman who lived in the turf house, and died a few weeks after she came up. Mrs. Alan had taken the baby, and was struggling to keep it alive, the house was very cold, she used to dress it up in flannel caps and mitts, when it went to bed, or it would have frozen. Her larder was very empty, all she could give us was dry bread, and some dried beef, very like a piece of shoe. All the poor baby had was bread and a scrape of butter, she had about 1/2 lb. and kept it just for the poor mite. We left early and that was the last of our gayities.

—*Mrs. John Willis*
A Start For The Great West
Circa 1880

Immigrant woman and child, Yorktown, Saskatchewan circa *1903*

Our trip from the Village of Camper, in 1914, to our homestead will remain in my memory forever. There was no road, only trails that wound through thick bush....I tried to remember some landmarks so I could find my way back to the station. I was certain that no human being could exist in this wilderness. By this time my husband had built a larger log house....There were eight of us, my in-laws, my mother, our three children, and my husband and myself. The house was all one room. Warm weather arrived, and with it came mosquitoes, flies and insects of every description. I had never witnessed anything like it. I thought to myself: "Before we die of loneliness the mosquitoes will eat us up, or perhaps even before that, the wolves that howl close by every night will mercifully end it all."

I carried on because...I had a secret that I revealed to no one. Upon my arrival, I knew I could not stay, so I tucked $10.00 away in a hiding place. As soon as my youngest child would be able to walk, I planned to take my children and my mother away, leaving this place to the wild animals. Surely my husband would give up this crazy idea of farming and follow. The ten dollars would be enough to pay fare back to Winnipeg.

That plan, however, was soon postponed. A baby was on its way. My determination to leave did not diminish, and as soon as the baby was old enough I would carry out the plan.

Our baby was still-born and my strength was slow in returning. My plan was delayed; but only until I was well and strong again. I looked at my ten dollars. After this summer, I must carry out my plan.

Autumn came, and my mind was occupied with plans of leaving. But, lo and behold, they had to be postponed again! Another baby would arrive in the Spring!...The desire to leave became even more intense. As soon as this baby arrived, I would not wait until it was old enough, I would take flight as soon as possible.

My eldest would have to walk three miles through bush and swamp to reach the school. No, I must not weaken! After the next baby is born, I must leave without a backward glance. I looked again at my ten dollars, carefully put another dollar next to it—and promised—*next time I shall not fail.*

My husband, who was a carpenter, helped to build homes for the other pioneers. In June, just before the baby came, he fell from the roof of a house he was building. He suffered broken ribs and an injured back, which confined him to bed for a long time. During this time, the baby arrived. It was a sickly one. Days were not long enough to look after him, tend my growing family, and do my husband's work. How could I leave now? I finally accepted defeat of my plan. I started to take a new interest in my home. Strangely enough, I did not seem to mind the howling of the wolves, the hooting of the owls nor the masses of mosquitoes. The ten dollars which I had secretly stowed away and carefully saved for my escape from this wilderness was no longer hidden. It was used to buy a plow!

—*"Mrs. Hoffman's Story"*
Pioneer Tales Of The Interlake

Harvesting potato crop, Manitoba, circa *1928*

II Life On The Prairie

Remember the CPR's vision of the ideal woman settler? a housekeeper, artist, poultry farmer, intellectual, dairywoman, humanitarian and gardener, all rolled into one. As unrealistic as the requirements may seem, pioneer farm women came close to fulfilling them. They were inspired to do so by the land itself, by its scope and promise for the future. But they were also motivated by the haunting prospect of crop-failure, starvation and defeat. Whenever their hope failed them, they were goaded on by necessity.

It was as if the prairie would tolerate the settlers' intrusion, but not without exacting its price. That much is evident from the operation of the homestead system. When a man came West, he was eligible for a "patent" that gave him the right to live and work on a particular quarter-section. If, at the end of three years, he had met certain residence and cultivation requirements, the land was his. Between 1870 and 1930, the government issued patents for 99,000,000 acres of prairie land, but it granted title to little more than half that amount. To put it in human terms, out of every ten people who optimistically set to work on a homestead, only six attained their dream. The prairie took its forfeit in energy and hope.

There were a number of reasons for the high failure rate. Although a few settlers were competent to take on the prairies, most of the newcomers—men and women alike—came poorly prepared for life on the frontier. What they couldn't do when they came, they often had to learn the hard way, by doing it wrong. Even those who had the necessary experience and skills seldom had enough cash to keep themselves afloat until their first profitable harvest. The immigration propaganda had implied that wheat seed in the ground was as good as money in the bank. In real life, where one had to cope with virgin land, fickle weather and exploitative grain handling agencies, there were likely to be several seasons of uncertainty and debt before the land began to pay.

Under these circumstances people were chronically short of cash with which to buy manufactured goods. As a result, they had to keep their purchases to a minimum by producing everything they could at home, whether it was a pound of lard or a cake of soap. In many cases, they also had to do without expensive labour savers like washing machines and running water. The settlers' first priority was not comfort but economic security: their future depended on making a commercial success of the farm. And any extra money was less likely to be spent on household conveniences than on efficient machinery for producing the cash crop. Consequently, the modernization of many households lagged far behind the mechanization of fieldwork. Long after the farm work had been taken over by horses and machines, many farm homes ran on womanpower.

For the typical pioneer woman, life was a hectic chorus of mend, weed, pump, chop, churn, bake and scrub. If she had children—and families tended to be large in those days—they added their giggles and howls. Until a schoolhouse was built, she might have to double as teacher and Mom. Even when she wasn't occupied directly by childcare she was often "in a family way". According to the wisdom of the day, a woman who rebelled against pregnancy was as absurd and irreverent as someone who rallied against death. The birth and death of babies was an unavoidable and sacred fact of nature. At that time, of course, contraception was socially and legally taboo, not the sort of thing that a polite and motherly woman tried to learn about. As late as 1925, birth control was still not being taught in all medical colleges, and until 1969, anyone who sold or advertised contraceptives in Canada ran the risk of being jailed for two years. If she were radical—or desperate—enough to consider birth control, the isolated farm woman had little access to information or advice. Whether she liked it or not, pregnancy generally followed fast upon childbirth.

The chances were poor that all of a woman's babies would survive. Even if the family could afford to pay medical bills, it probably couldn't get professional care. Doctors and hospitals were few and far between. For the most part, Mother had to manage on her own, diagnosing illnesses with the help of a well-thumbed "doctor book" and administering her home-made remedies. In most communities, a family could occasionally call in a practical nurse or midwife, a neighbourhood woman who volunteered her services during childbirth or an emergency. Although some of these women lacked formal training, many of them became highly skilled. Working under primitive conditions in pioneer shacks, they did what they could, not out of a sense of heroism but because it had to be done by someone, and there was no one else around.

Isolation was one of the overwhelming factors in a pioneer woman's life. Although a number of immigrants came to Canada in community groups, most farms were established by individual families. Since the government only permitted homesteading on alternate sections of land, initial settlement was thinly scattered. It might be two or three miles between farmsteads. Because of the size of the "spreads", the problem was particularly acute in the ranchlands. A visit to the neighbours could be a major outing. With so much work to be done, and so few women to do it, there simply wasn't much time for fun. The less frequently women were able to get together, the more they seem to have valued one another's company and assistance.

As a rule, the men were much more mobile. If anyone left the farmstead on business, they were usually the ones to go. If anyone took a seasonal job away from home, it was generally the men; the women were left on the farm to manage alone. Because of their contact with the outside community, the men were the first to make friends and to learn English, if that wasn't the family's mother tongue. According to the census figures for 1916, immigrant women in all ethnic communities were slower to pick up the new language than the men. The most extreme case was that of Ukrainian-born women in Saskatchewan, of whom fewer than 20% could speak English.

Distance, custom and cultural barriers were not all that kept women apart. The most powerful force was work. In addition to the house, children and health care, Mother was often responsible for the farmyard too. The garden, chicken coop and barn were generally her domain. The sales of her poultry, butter and eggs were often an important source of income during the first debt-burdened seasons on a homestead, and one of the few reliable sources for years to come. As if that were not enough, she generally did field work as well, labouring alongside the men. Obviously, women carried much of the responsibility for the day-to-day survival of the family, and helped to build its long-range prosperity as well.

At the very least, prairie women bore their share, yet their legal and financial status did not reflect this contribution. By 1900, female taxpayers in Manitoba were voting in municipal and school elections, but they could not hold office. Women had no direct input into provincial, territorial or federal politics. They were not eligible to serve on juries or to act as the legal guardians of their children. Unless they were solely responsible for a family, they could not qualify for a homestead in their own name. While a woman could manage her own property and income, a wife had no claim to money she earned on a farm owned by her husband. Regardless of how much labour she put into acquiring the land and making it pay, if it was registered in her husband's name, she had no control over its mortgage or sale, and no certainty of an inheritance in her old age. A married woman on the prairies had the responsibilities of an adult partner and the legal status of a child. It was inconsistent, it was unfair, it was hard to bear; but, for the most part, women bided their peace during the first few years. Nellie McClung was probably right in saying that they were simply too busy to complain.

How vividly I recall my first day on the farm, and the almost overwhelming realization it brought me of my total lack of knowledge of the kind of life that lay ahead of me.

—*Katherine Strange*
With The West In Her Eyes

You did everything by hand, everything the hard way, and I think the women... did just as much to make this western country as any of the men did. They were just taken for granted—that was their job, they were supposed to do that. Men, of course, they got blowed up about what they did. They were supposed to do theirs too but they got talked about where the women didn't. Women sat in the background while the men got praised.

—*Mrs. Inez Hendersen*
Hythe, Alberta
Interview, 1974

HOW WE DO OUR OWN WORK ON A FARM

Living as we do on a farm, the size of our family varies. Probably four would be a fair average—all adults. We have eight rooms. The only woman in the family, I do all the work. This includes washing, scrubbing, butter-making and house cleaning. It is always difficult and usually impossible to get a woman for even a few hours, and I depend upon my own efforts rather than attempt to find help.

I buy bread only in an emergency; all other food is prepared at home. Among my household treasures are a washing machine, a bread-mixer, a food chopper and a carpetsweeper—and they are all indispensable.

So far as possible I try to conform to this schedule: Monday, washing; Tuesday, ironing; Wednesday, baking; Thursday, sweeping upstairs; Friday, sweeping downstairs; Saturday, baking.

—*Gertrude Stewart Hyde*
Grain Growers' Guide
September 11, 1909

Women sawing

Washing! What a job that always was. Usually it took me the entire day. In summer I washed outside; in winter, down in the basement. The boiling, sudsy water had to be carried in pails from the stove to wherever my tubs were set. More than once I burned myself severely, spilling water on unprotected hands and legs.

I washed for the hired men as well as for my own family. We were always from eight to fifteen strong, according to the time of the year, and since most of the men worked in close contact with the soil, and with animals, there was always an astonishing pile of extremely dirty clothing—mountains of overalls and socks, heavy underwear and flannel shirts, not to speak of voluminous bed linen.

Drying the clothes was almost as much of a job as washing them, especially in winter. It often took the best part of a week, and for many months during the year, when the weather was cold, the various rooms of our house were made uncomfortable and unpleasant with smelly underwear and clumsy flannel shirts which took not hours but days to air thoroughly.

—*Katherine Strange*
With The West In Her Eyes

HOME REMEDIES FOR BUGS

Being once troubled with bed bugs, I know how to sympathize with anyone who has them. I had tried various cures but to no avail, when one day my daughter came in and said, "Mother, your troubles are over. I have a cure for bed bugs." The cure was gasoline. So I bought two gallons. I gave my bedsteads, mattresses and every place where I thought they could get a good soaking twice. The gasoline hurts nothing, if you keep it away from fires. Be very careful of a blaze, or you will rue ever having used it for it is very inflammable.

Well, I used the gasoline in this way five years ago, and I have never seen a bug since.

———————

I notice in *The Guide* someone inquiring for something to kill bed bugs. Well, I could not refrain from writing to tell you what I know, so that it may benefit anyone tormented as I once was in a house I moved into in Moose Jaw. I tried everything I could hear tell of but with no real satisfaction until a person told me to use sheep dip. Take a half-cup of sheep dip to a quart of warm water. With a good stiff feather go into all the crevices. This will not injure bedding, so you can apply freely. One or two applications will rid your house forever. You can get this at any drug store.

—Grain Growers' Guide
circa 1915

Laundry

Fort Edmonton
August 28, 1879

My Own Dear Mother:

Since the last time I wrote you we have got comfortable settled. We rented a nice large house until our own is finished they are buisy building it but I hardly think it will be done before spring. The house we have rented is very nice. The stoar is up stairs and we live down I have 4 large rooms sitting room bedroom kitchen and a large hall. It is not plastered but finished of very nice it is all wood work. I had to scour it all. My carpet just fits my sitting room.I have lace and blue damask curtains to the windows some nice pictures and the organ, table for my books and one we eat on. We have not many chairs but 2 good ones and I covered a little box with damask. So my room looks splendid Johnnie is going to make a lounge this week. In my kitchen I have shelves for my dishes and we use the organ box for a table Henry eats in the kitchen. I have no cooking stove yet so I have great times cooking by the fire place. I find it so unhandy but Johnnie is getting 2 stoves from Winnipeg this fall I bake in the frying pan and I am baking all the time. But Mrs. Coleman one of the white women here is going to set a batch of bread for me tonight and I will bake it in her stove she lives not far from us.

…We have a nice little cow we bought from Mr. Walton but I have not made any butter yet as I had no place to keep the milk so we gave it to the calf….This week I had a halfbreed woman washing my bed clothes they are all dry now and put away. I changed the feathers into the new bed tick this week to all the things I brought from home are as good as ever. I did not use them before. Today Johnnie bought 2 pails of huckleberries. I intend to preserve some and use the rest for pies. I bake pies in a bake kettle and they are splendid….I get along splendid house keeping I like it. And I do not find it a bit dull up here. Their are lots of people comming and going all the time. Their are only four white women here besides myself. Two of them called on me but the other two are Hudson Bay officers wives and the Hudson Bay Company is vexed at Johnnie for selling cheaper than they do so I don't expect the wives will call on me. When the new Minister comes I expect to have a nice friend in his wife. Last week Johnnie took me out to Big Lake the Catholic Mission. We had dinner with the Nuns they were very nice they have a beautifull flower garden they gave me a nice boquet. I was asking them about making butter they make splendid butter I bought some from them. They told me to wash it in cold water after I took it out of the churn untill all the milk was out is that the way you do. I wish you would tell me all you can about it please.

Louisa Jane McDougall

Typical farm kitchen among Scandinavian-American settlers, Marchwell, Saskatchewan, 1906

We had our own garden. We grew everything that you want to buy: potatoes, carrots, beans, radishes and so on. And we stored these in the root house in the winter time. My mother used to supply not only ourselves but the whole community. When town people came to visit you'd entertain them by showing your garden. Mother would take them around. She was so proud of the rows of onions and cabbages and everything else she grew. She wouldn't let anyone leave without taking home a big bunch of vegetables.

—*Ada Silverton*
Wapella Farm Settlement

Housekeeping in the early days required inventive genius. Children arrived and brought added work with them; why I've carried the little ones to the fence corner, made them as comfortable as possible and then helped stack hay, stook grain, build fences and harrow the ploughed fields, having done my housework and churning before coming out.

Taking a tea break, Gladstone, Manitoba, 1916

This log house, mud plastered, I helped to build with my own hands....it took four years to qualify for a homestead patent, for my husband and the boys big enough to work, had to leave home and hire out, leaving me with the young children to "hold down" the farm....just as we got on our feet, my husband died, leaving us alone....I just buckled to and kept on, running the farm with the boys' help. Butter making and vegetable raising and poultry raising proved the best cash returns, I found, so I stuck to that leaving the boys to seed, grow and harvest the grain.

—Women's Work In Western Canada
C.P.R. propaganda booklet
1906

The want of household and field help is the only bug bear in farm life. I myself have for six seasons ridden the binder beside my husband, who handled the other and I can do my 15 acres in a day too! I do this work because men are scarce and getting the crop off the field is a first thought. I do all my own housework, besides milking a dozen cows, churning and making every week a hundred pounds of butter for market.

Threshing crew, Foremost, Alberta, 1917

Father would never stick a pig nor even kill a chicken. He always had a neighbor come to kill the pigs, and mother used to wring the necks of the chickens. She didn't like doing it any better than he did, but she was realistic and if we were going to eat, someone had to do the deed. She did it as she did many unpleasant things that had to be done. I can't remember father doing anything he didn't want to do.

Once the pigs were killed mother had more hard jobs to do. The lard had to be rendered, a greasy, smelly job, but we all enjoyed the pies and other good things made with it afterwards.

—*Georgina H. Thomson*
Crocus & Meadowlark Country

You know I was the veterinary on the farm and everything else....He was no good at that at all and so if any animal got sick it was me.

Oh I can remember helping a young heifer with her calf. She couldn't have it...and I knew my husband was gone...When he went, he didn't come back for awhile. And I saw her getting up and laying down and getting up and laying down and I took a rope (I don't know how I ever happened to take this rope) and I went down and I pulled her calf. But it died you know. I didn't get there in time to save it. But I saved the heifer, yes, I sure did.

And I used to take care if something happened to the cow. They'd get these big...abscesses sometimes when they'd get hurt. It was always me that doctored those abscesses. They used to call me the veterinary. I never learned from anybody. I just wasn't afraid and I just didn't have the money.

I remember one of our expensive holstein heifers. He set the dog on it, and she ran between the shed and the tractor. Her bag flopped and she run a sliver in her bag...But I didn't know it at the time and she got thinner and her milk went down. So I felt in her bag and there was this great big abscess and I thought, what am I going to do? I went to the house and I got a crochet hook and I went to the grindstone and I just ground it down to a fine point and I put that in the abscess and bathed her in hot water and salts and she...got better.

And then there were the horses. We thought so much of this team, we called them Robbie and Nan...I saw Nan was just in agony. And I took a great big heavy quilt and I heated the tub full of hot water and I went out and I dipped this big quilt into the hot water. I don't know how I ever got it on her but I remember getting a box to stand on so that I'd be tall enough and I kept that over her back and you know, she acted as though it just felt so good...You could see that old horse was just appreciating everything that was being done for her.... Anyway, I kept doing this the best I could, no way to get hot water but on the cook stove, but I kept pots and pans and everything full and I saved my horse.

—*Mrs. Mae Olstad*
Camrose, Alberta
Interview, 1975

Woman tending horses, St. Peter's Abbey, Muenster, Saskatchewan, 1912

By unfriendly critics, much has been made of the fact that the Doukhobor women perform the arduous work of harnessing themselves to the plough, but this is entirely at their own suggestion.

At first the women were greatly in the majority, as their fathers, sons, and husbands were in Siberian exile, and much of the work had, therefore, to be done by the womenfolk. It was when only a few draught horses were available, and these were needed to haul logs from a distance so that homes might be built before the rigours of winter set in, that the women volunteered, with true Spartan fortitude, to break up the land.

———————

The Doukhobor woman is a housewife. She does not believe that her home is a jail, and that her babies are the turnkeys. Like Solomon's virtuous woman, she "seeketh wool and flax, and worketh willingly with her hands."

On the other hand, she is a housewife only. She is not expected, as our Anglo-Saxon women are, to be a combination of Mary, Martha, Magdalen, Bridget, and the Queen of Sheba.

—*Emily Ferguson*
Janey Canuck In The West

Doukhobour women at work

She had a nice home. Forget the rest—the heartache, the doubts and the fears, the uncertain looking into the future and the wondering why it must be—which came after she had been stripped of husband, father-in-law, two lovely little girls and a boy of more than ordinary promise.

She was ten miles from market. All she had after the wreck was a little place of sixty acres, not very well equipped for business.

"You will have to give it up, won't you?" was the question which came to her from her friends. It was the thing most women who had been left in that situation would have done.

"I am not going to give up." This is the answer she made to her friends. After all, it was her home, and she said she did not want to live anywhere else.

"But how can you stay? What will you do? There is no one to do the work. You had better close up the house and go back to your father's...."

Never very strong and now troubled with a bronchial infection, it seemed like an impossibility that she could have done what she has. The first thing was to get some good cows on the farm.... Not being able to buy thoroughbred cows, she began with what she had, and by breeding from the best stock available and selecting calves of the most promising parentage she has gathered about her some of the most productive cows of the neighborhood....

She has milked the mother cow herself and taken care of them, feeding them, getting the hay down from the mow alone; with her skirts tucked up she has done a man's work in the stables and actually attended to all that had to be done about the barns.

Then this woman of heroic heart took the milk down to the house and set it in the old-fashioned way in open pans and turned it into butter that was fit for a queen to eat.

Some of the most particular people in a city of forty or fifty thousand are eating that butter every year and paying her the top price for it. Now, what if one should say, "Oh, well, she is a strong, man-like woman. Of course she could not be very refined or cultured, or she would never think of doing these things." You, who sit in your parlors, with all you need to make you happy around you, plenty of money and all that heart can wish, stop and listen. I doubt if you could hold your own in a conversation upon the current events of the day with this queen of the farm. The best papers, daily, weekly, and monthly, come to her home. She does not feel that everything is right unless she has found time before she goes to bed to sit down and see what has been going on in the world outside....She is posted on the markets as to the price of all farm products in which she is particularly interested. She markets her pork and sells her eggs when they will sell to the best advantage.

And there she is. Shut in? Not at all. In need of pity? Far from it. She is worthy of the highest admiration and she gets it from all who know her.

—Edgar L. Vincent
"Victory From Defeat"
Grain Growers' Guide

Woman churning butter, Springfield Ranch, Beynon, Alberta, circa *1908*

I no longer utter a mental protest against the prairie as a final resting place. Our western life is too real, too vital to waste time in gloomy speculation. It is enough that you are alive and can take your chances in the great future that lies just at hand.

—Gertrude Watt
A Woman In The West

I was married when I was about 19. I raised a family of five children, three boys and two girls and that's when the work begins. After I got married I really worked and of course you don't get married and raise a family and not work because there's something wrong if you don't. But you know I liked it. It was a very plain life and I was only too happy.

—Mrs. Mae Olstad
Camrose, Alberta
Interview, 1975

We are quite happy and contented, very much better off than we were in England, whilst as to good we live quite as well as ever we did....

Certainly we have had difficulties to surmount and hardships to endure but we quite expected we should before we left England and we treasured up a reserve fund of determination and pluck which stood us in good stead when the need came. I would never advise anyone to come out here who is the least afraid of work, they are better off at home. There is plenty of room to breathe in this country and if the work is hard the freedom, which is the indispensable attribute of the life here, makes one far less susceptible to physical fatigue than in England where one seems to have such a feeling of weighty oppression to handicap one's energies. Here one feels that each week's work is a step onward whilst alas in the old country oftentimes a year's hard toil brought nothing but disappointment and additional anxiety.

—Mrs. Rendell, Barr Colonist
Letter Home To England

Mabel Mazey was the friendliest person....All her days she worked in the open air and loved it. In herding cattle, tending young stock, ploughing, discing, harrowing, she was equally useful, happy and at home; but she was a true daughter of the four winds of the prairie, and often have I listened to argument as to which is the most rousing way of the wind in Canada—north, south, east or west. She didn't jump at the idea of coming over once a week to break the back of my domestic duties.

—Georgina Binnie-Clark
Wheat And Woman

Horseback rider, Alberta

Life was very monotonous in the winter, and very lonely. One year there were seven months that they never saw a woman or girl, outside of their own family circle. At times the loneliness grew almost unbearable to the girls. Every book that was interesting was read over and over again. Then their father's library was hunted through, but the medical works were set aside as too deep, besides their father did not wish them to be touched, but among his books were found Flavius Josepheus and "Fox's Book of Martyrs," which kept them reading for a long while. A neighbor sent some books over one winter and among them was one called "Charles O'Malley." The girls enjoyed very much when they read of the Peninsular War which is so graphically described in it, they asked their mother so many questions, that she told them to hunt it up in the British History, which they did and soon were passionately fond of history of all kinds, and eagerly read any book they could get on historical subjects. The same story aroused their curiosity in regard to the location of the different countries, and cities named in it, so a geography was purchased and the places hunted for on the maps, then the descriptions of each read, so that they were receiving an education though they could not go to school.

During the long, cold winter, it seemed that all our effort and energy were spent in just keeping alive...but when the spring came life seemed to take on deeper meaning, and we felt we were a part, even if a small one, of a greater purpose of awakening, of creation and of growth.

—*Sarah Ellen Roberts*
Of Us And Oxen

Homestead, Lloydminster area, circa *1910*

Once I visited another of the early settlers. She was a young woman with a baby and she was lonely too. She had come from Utah with her husband who was trying to farm but being a city boy it was hard work for him. When we met, we ran to each other; we each had to speak to a woman, and put our arms around each other's neck and just had a good cry. All the hunger and longing which we had stifled for so long, came to the surface. We felt better after our cry.

When I told her I was going to have a baby, she gave me patterns for nighties and bands and told me how to make a barrowcoat. I felt after that visit that I could go through anything now that I had a friend to go to in need. Her home was several miles from the ranch, but I managed to visit her sometimes.

—*Catherine Neil*
"One Big Family"
The Western Producer

One summer afternoon mother went on another visiting trip...to a neighbor who lived only two miles away. The occasion was quite an event, for it was the first time that she had been off the farm since the two year old twins were born. In the first place, she couldn't very well take them both with her at one time while they were tiny babies and secondly, the children in the home were too young for the twins to be left in their charge.

Welcoming visitors

We always had a succession of visitors on Sunday afternoons. In order to provide for these possible guests, in addition to our own family, I used to stock up with plenty of meat, potatoes, pie, cake and fruit. I would cook a roast sometimes as big as twenty to thirty pounds on Saturday morning. I would peel a pail full of potatoes. I would bake a big batch of bread, two large cakes, numerous cookies, and at least six pies. The house would be given a general clean over, the kitchen well scrubbed, and everything placed in readiness for the morrow.This meant that Sunday would be as nearly a day of rest as we farm people could ever make it.

—*Katherine Strange*
With The West In Her Eyes

What should hinder us from enjoying each other's society? It is true that we do not scatter cards upon each other, or make many afternoon calls, by reasons of time and space and other large consideration. We do not give each other dinner parties either; but we give each other dinner, generally at 1 p.m., and beds for the night. People usually come when they have some reason for passing this way; and in a ranching country, nurses are so few and far between that hospitality of necessity becomes a matter of course. As a matter of course, also, people do not expect to be amused.

—*High River Pioneers' & Old Timers' Association*
Leaves From The Medicine Tree

They made it all! The women were the ones that made the good times. The men, all they did was sit around and yak.

—*Mrs. Inez Hendersen*
Hythe, Alberta
Interview, 1974

Community gathering

There was no telephone to get in touch with the doctor. The only thing you could do was to send somebody on horseback—to get the doctor. But, of course if the roads were bad, he probably never got there. He'd start but he wouldn't get there, so she'd have to gather up her courage and do what she never did before.

—Mrs. Rogers
Past President, Alberta Women's Institute
Interview, 1974

The only doctor was the police doctor at Fort Macleod. Mrs. Morden, who came from Ontario and settled with her husband where the town of Pincher Creek is now, wisely learned how to pull teeth before leaving Ontario, and being a strong woman she eased toothaches with her forceps.

—Fred W. Godsal

Spring came again, and May: a year had passed and I had not looked upon the face of a white woman since I came.

Cowboys, ranchers galore, came to talk, and to fill their empty stomachs but not a woman dawned on my horizon till glory be! my little Irish neighbor with a kind heart, and ready wit, who was to live eight miles up the river, came upon the scene, with her big husband and three small children! I shall never forget the joy of seeing a woman's face again. Upon my asking her what we were going to do if we needed a Doctor, she laughed and said, "Shure we'll have to dope each other," which we did on more than one occasion.

—Saskatchewan Homesteading Experiences

I used a lot of home remedies. The first thing I did when I went on the homestead was pay $10 for a doctor book. And all those little ailments children get, I took care of, because we lived 15 miles from town and travelled by horses. When you had sick children, you could kill them just by taking them on that trip.

—Mrs. Elizabeth Akitt
Edmonton, Alberta
Interview, 1973

THE PRAIRIE WIFE
Far from Medical Aid

From the Calgary Eye-Opener, *July 8, 1916*

Castor oil, liniment and cod-liver oil, quinine, beef and iron tonic and various salves were about all the shelves contained. With Dr. Chevasse's medical book to guide her, my mother would diagnose and treat an illness to the best of her ability....My brother Don was what Mother called a "croupy child". He would go to bed as healthy as a trout and suddenly in the night we would hear his ominous coughing....Her cure was to give the unfortunate little fellow half a teaspoon of coal-oil, which she would take from one of the lamps. In larger doses I'm sure it would be lethal, but nevertheless it did alleviate his breathing.

My mother rubbed a congested chest with goose oil....She used soda for bites and cold tea leaves for burns; salt in water to gargle a sore throat; senna tea for a laxative and "ippecaka" or sulphur and molasses for a spring tonic. Above all she was always serene and after listening to our complaints, if we felt out of sorts, would invariably say, "Well, we'll see how it is in the morning"....There was many a night when she watched by our bedsides until a fever broke or some other minor crisis passed and many a prayer she breathed on our behalf.

—Gladys L. Allan (née Lamb)
Dew On The Grass

REMEDY FOR SORE BREASTS

Boil half a cup of brandy with a little sunlight in Royal Crown soap shredded fine, and whilst warm lather the breasts well with it, round under the arms as well. Next day wash off with warm water and repeat the brandy and soap and wash again. Be sure and put some good warm covering over the breasts and keep them warm. The nurse did mine twice and I never had an hours pain after. Since coming to this country I have tried it on four women and it never failed.

—Grain Growers' Guide
April 29, 1914

With the last two pregnancies I also used considerable slippery elm, always carrying a piece in my pocket and chewing a bit whenever I felt like eating between meals. I tried to eat sparingly all through the period and found it handy to have something like that to keep me from wanting to eat too often.

I made a thin slippery tea of the flax seed and drank it off quite a few times each day, putting on more water to keep it from getting too thick and slimy. If some of the seeds go down, too, there is no harm done. It is well worth trying, this slippery elm and flax seed regime, also the sparing diet. I got some of these ideas from a book called "Tohology" which will be found invaluable to wives and mothers.

—Grain Growers' Guide
January 21, 1914

A one-room home, Winnipeg (from the Annual Report of Neglected Children for the Province of Manitoba 1912)

I am a mother of 5 children, the oldest being 7 years. I am 25 years old. We live on the farm, but owing to sickness we haven't got on very well. I trust we will do better soon, as debts are a very constant worry....
Please send information on birth control.

—*"Another Reader"*
The Western Producer
November 10, 1927

I am 31, the mother of 7 children, eldest 11 years, and youngest 8 months, not at all strong, and owing to farm conditions, very heavily in debt. I would like to have any information I can get re birth control.

—*Mrs. E.J.M.*
The Western Producer
September 29, 1927

Dear Mamma:
I received your letter last night, the first for a couple of weeks. I rather thought your call came earlier than expected. Am glad she's all right even if it was a girl....So you wanted some information. Well, I can tell you several different methods. I have the real recipe of that cocoa butter....A friend's...sister...got from her doctor after she'd had four. He charged her $50 for it, but since, she's given it to dozens and it works. It's just 1 lb. cocoa butter and 1 oz. of common boric acid and 1 1/2...oz. of Tannic acid. It's a powder like boric acid only yellowish. You put the three in a sauce pan over hot water and the coca butter will melt. Then stir it all together and pour 1/2 inch thick in a pie-pan and cool. When cool cut in 1/2 inch squares like fudge. It smells good enough to eat. Then before each time put one of those pieces up there and it will melt at body heat in a minute or so. Coca butter alone is a preventive and so is tannic acid and these absolutely won't harm. I have my own doctor's word for that. I have some made and will send it by this parcel....I don't see why it should'nt be good, even if it has stood. I guess there are any number of ways...I knew a woman in Buffalo who had a dear friend. She had a mean jealous husband. They had two girls and he made his brag that he'd see that his wife never got the chance to run around. Said there would be kids in his house every year. He'd keep his brag. This was 25 years ago and those things were'nt so popular so she said she'd fix him. So she took a good sized of sponge and soaked it with soap suds and put it up next the uterus. It worked for her and he never knew. As soon as she could do so, without arousing his suspicions she would take it out and douche. I don't see why it would'nt do, but use water with a few drops of some antiseptic or even plain vinegar. I also know several other ways but don't like to encourage anyone without more definite information about them....

—*Undated, unsigned typescript in Violet McNaughton's personal papers*

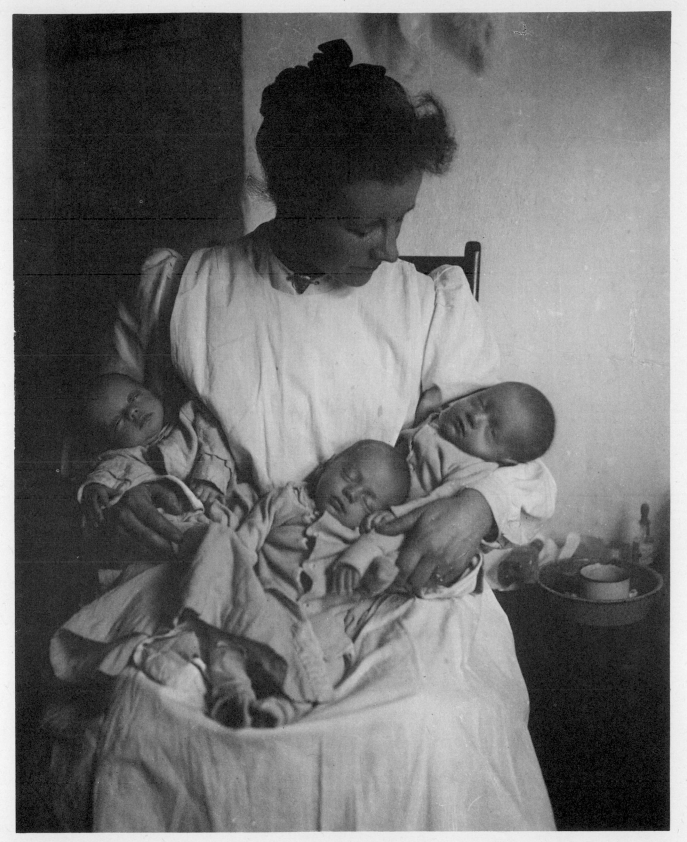

Three of the Robertson quadruplets, 1907

No, we never thought about it... [birth control] at all. If you got that way you got that way and there was no such thing as abortion because that was like taking a life, you see. I've known some people who brought it on themselves and they've suffered quite a lot by it. You know, they put the knitting needles in them and try to break the womb open.

And then they were sick and had to have a doctor of course that didn't give them any comfort....the best way was not to bother with nature at all, you see. When we had hard times we used to say we should of thought about this and controlled ourselves more and not have had a large family, but we didn't do those things.

—*Mrs. Beatrice Vincent (née Haskell)*
Interview, January 1975

Despite the fact that I had always regarded myself as a very modern young woman, and had known about most of the "facts of life" long before I was married, I actually knew little or nothing about the physical phenomena of human pregnancy and birth.

I had no intimate friends at that time from whom to seek advice or sympathy, so that, as the time passed and my condition became physically apparent, I began to feel very bewildered, and sometimes terribly frightened, at the prospect of what was going to happen to me. I knew moments of almost breathless happiness and anticipation, but there were also long periods of intense discomfort, boredom and fear.

—*Katherine Strange*
With The West In Her Eyes

Even with the high infant mortality, the Ukrainians are still well in advance of the British when it comes to the size of the family....The children come as a matter of course, and they come frequently.

Now and then the women rebel—and then it is quite common for doctors to get requests to perform abortions, this, usually owing to the physical disability of the women. One doctor remarked: "If you only knew the number of women who come here with tears in their eyes asking for relief."

While requests for abortion are frequent, birth control is practically unknown except among the younger generation and even among them not to any great extent.

—*Charles H. Young*
The Ukrainian-Canadians

Children, Lloydminster area

All the Icelandic midwives deserve special mention but one of them, Gudrun Goodman, had one experience, while still a young woman, which stands out as the finest example of courage and initiative in an emergency. A young woman was with child, expecting in about a week. She was pumping water for a team of oxen who were drinking out of a low trough. Both the oxen had long sharp horns. One of them suddenly raised its head and one of the horns caught the woman in the side and ripped it open. Gudrun Goodman was immediately summoned. She saw that she could not save the woman but was determined to save the child. She administered an anesthetic, chloroform, operated and got the child while still alive. She brought it up—Guobjorg Eyjolkfson, who later became Mrs. Thomas Halldorson, of Leslie, Saskatchewan.

—*Walter (Valdimar) Jacobson Lindal*
The Saskatchewan Icelanders

After awhile our family begin to come along...I'd never had a doctor ever since I'd come from England...to Canada and then it wasn't because I wanted to, but ...because they told me I should....They told us you'll have to have a doctor and...a midwife....So we sent for one and they was three hours late and I had everything done, had the baby dressed and myself washed and the afterbirth taken out and put into the heater. And then he came and felt my pulse and said, "Well you're just as nature led you. That's forty-five dollars please." Yes, that was it and he'd only come six miles....But I had sent for him and naturally I had to pay him. So after that when I was in a family way I never sought for any doctor. I asked the Lord to help me and he gave me health and strength. I had all twelve of them without any doctor or woman....But I will say, at this time, I saw an advertisement in the *Free Press* about Indians using herbs to cut down labor pains and they were a dollar a box. So I thought, well I'll send for a box anyway. And as soon as labor pains started I took a cupful of these herbs that was steeped in water and that took out all the labor pains....And the last baby that was born, I stood up and caught him in my arms and laid him on the bed and reached over and got the scissors and separated the cord. Then I got a bowl of warm water and washed him and fixed up myself.

—*Mrs. Beatrice Vincent (née Haskell)*
Interview, January, 1975

Women of Didsbury, Alberta, 1911

Marriages and births were not uncommon in those days, and many a little stranger was ushered into this world without either a doctor's or nurses' care. A very sad part too as very many precious lives went out, that might have been spared had there been experienced help on hand. Many a coffin hid the face of both mother and infant.

—Saskatchewan Homesteading Experiences

I had a doctor. I never had anyone to stay with me after my baby was born, but I had a doctor, and I had a nurse. She was a nurse who had come from the old country where she'd been trained in nursing and midwifery. If I hadn't had her when my youngest son was born I would have been dead. We had a doctor who wouldn't take any notice of what she said, even though she'd had good training in the old country....She must have been about 55 then. She saved my life, because the doctor told my husband he couldn't save me. I was really sick but she did the trick, she knew what to do. She said she told him 2 hours before my baby was born that she could do it if he let her. And he did let her. He said "You take the consequences." I know what lots of women have gone through by not having a doctor. Sometimes there was just a neighbor; no midwife.

My neighbor who used to live just across here died because she couldn't get to a hospital to have her baby. You have to be pretty strong to take that kind of thing.

—Mrs. Elizabeth Akitt
Edmonton, Alberta
Interview, 1973

Mama had never been strong and Papa and we children had always done what we could to spare her...Privations which we took as a matter of course must have been deeply felt by her, but she never complained and made the best of what was at hand. While she seldom went away from home, she was always ready to help, and on many occasions went to the assistance of neighbors who were ill and in need. She worked far beyond her strength and the cares and difficulties of pioneer life must have been harder for her to bear than we realized.

About the middle of December, Mama took a heavy cold and it rapidly grew worse...She passed away just as the doctor entered...Neighbors came with helpful sympathy. She was buried in sight of the house on a knoll up on the bench, a spot she and Papa had already chosen as a family burying-ground...

If my record of Mama's death is short, it is only because its memory, after all these years, still causes too keen a regret that she, whose life was spent for others, should pass away so young. She was forty-five and had borne ten children.

—Account of Pioneer Life

An early death

All in all we were happy, though I know it must have been terrible for Mother who was again expecting the stork, and with no one else in the vast wilderness nearer than Fort Ellice, twenty miles away, shut in by deep snow drifts, in a log cabin about 12X16, with bunks built against one wall, a cook stove in one corner, a table and the sewing machine in the other and the box stove in the centre, yet even in those close quarters Mother kept us clean and did the chores, fed the stock and chickens, and milked the cows, until one morning in early spring I awakened to a cry of a new-born baby. Child though I was I recognized...it for that, and immediately after I heard Father say, "Oh Bella, there's another mouth to feed." No word of sympathy for her suffering nor any sign that it was she who carried the heavy end of the load; well, she of course did not get any care...Things drifted on for a couple of years with Mother and Father quarrelling most of the time and she'd go and stay...with first one and then another, sewing and helping one way and another to just be out of the turmoil. Then she had another attack of delerium and during an awful time Father took her to Moosomin and had her sent to Brandon to the government hospital for incurables...

After 7 or 8 years in the institution Mother having been well all the time and working as hard as any of the paid attendants of the institution, found a way to return and try to gather up her children....Then Father was working in Moosomin and she went there to see him. He was not to be found and while she was waiting for him a man...lost his wife and was left with a large family of small children. Mother went first just to help them out, later to keep house for him, until Father should return and they could gather up their scattered family. That was her hope. Well, Father came there to see her... and of course the usual result was achieved and poor Mother was again expecting a child; that was Lawrence...she went to work for the Harris house in Moosomin. She worked there till a few weeks before the baby was born. Father having finished the job he was on, came there to the Hotel....Mother was working all the time so they took a trip out to Browns' and Davis', from there to Wakefield's to see all the rest of we children and coming back to Moosimin to the Harris house a short time before the baby was expected with poor Mother no nearer the home she wanted than before....The baby was born a week sooner than the necessary nine months since he had visited Mother where she was working so he immediately disowned it and went off to Vancouver to work on the C.P.R....leaving her with a board bill of his and her doctor bill to settle, and no money to do it with. Then Mrs. Harris got impatient and when Mother wanted to go and work somewhere to get money to follow Father, held her clothes and the baby's also for back board. The inevitable happened as soon as she tried to get clear; and what person would not be in a mad rage at such injustice. She was again bundled off to the institution with the baby, where she stayed until her death, with typhoid fever, five years later.

—*Lizzie Johnson*
Story Of A Cruel Father

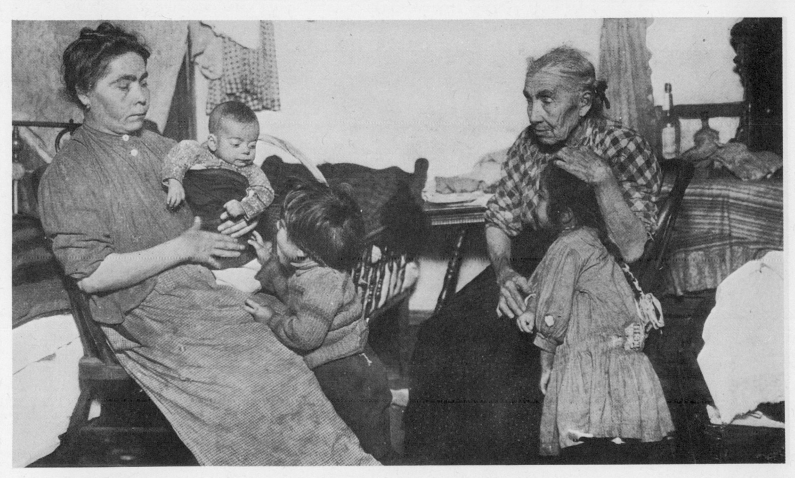

Métis family

And why not a holiday for the country woman, pray? Her city sister, who has only one bairn and keeps a maid, is off, with the first hot weather to the lakes, while the country mother with a big family and no help only speeds up a little harder during the summer months. The city woman complains that after the long, strenuous winter her nerves are all in rags. The country woman's nerves are probably in veritable tatters but she never complains about it...She simply could not be spared from home for a holiday. The whole place would go to rack and ruin, she believes, in her absence....If there is a weakness peculiar to the feminine sex I believe it is the tendency to make martyrs of themselves unecessarily. Compared to sound bodies and sound minds, what matters the acquisition of a few acres of land or the increase of flocks and herds? And yet it is just this very sordid consideration which keeps many a woman at her post long after common sense tells her it is time to quit and take a rest.

—Grain Growers' Guide
July 14, 1915

On the farms before electricity and labor-saving devices lightened their loads, women's work obsessed them. Their hours were endless, their duties imperative. Many broke under the strain and died, and their places were filled without undue delay. Some man's sister or sister-in-law came from Ontario to take the dead woman's place. Country cemeteries bear grim witness to the high mortality rate in young women.

—*Nellie McClung*
The Stream Runs Fast

Heather Brae, Alberta
January 12, 1906

Miss Jennie Magee
Dear Sister:
You will be surprised to hear from me after so many years. Well I have bad news for you. My Dear little wife is Dead and I am the lonelyist Man in all the world. She gave Birth to little Daughter on the 27th of December three Days after she went out of her mind and on the 7th of January she took Pnumonia and Died about half past three in the afternoon. We buried her tuesday afternoon in a little cemetary on the Prarry about 15 miles from here. I am writing to you to see if you will come and keep house for me and raise my little Baby. I would not like to influence you in any way as I am afraid you would be lonely when I have to go from home as I will now and again. You are used to so much stir in the city. I have 400 acres of Land and I have 9 or ten cows and some hens. If you come you can make all you can out of the Butter and eggs and I might be able to Pay you a small wage...Write and let me know as soon as Possible what you think about the Proposition. I am writing to the rest tonight to let them know the bad news. I think this is all at Present from your affectionate Brother.

William Magee

Haying, Foley, Manitoba, circa *1903*

"Born an' scrubbed, suffered an' died."
That's all you need to say, elder.
Never mind sayin' "made a bride,"
Nor when her hair got gray.
Jes' say "born 'n worked t' death";
That fits it—save y'r breath.

          —Hamlin Garland
           "The Farmer's Wife"
           The Saskatchewan

NO OCCUPATION

She rose before daylight made crimson the east
For duties that never diminished.
And never the sun when it sank in the west
Looked down upon work that was finished.
She cooked an unending procession of meals,
Preserving and canning and baking.
She swept and she dusted,
She washed and she scrubbed,
With never a rest from it taking
A family of children she brought in the world.
Raised them and trained them and taught them.
She made all the clothes and patched, mended and darned
'Til miracles seemed to have wrought them.
She watched by the bedside of sickness and pain
Her hand cooled the raging of fever.

Carpentered, painted, upholstered and scrapped
And worked just as hard as a beaver.
And yet as a lady-of-leisure, it seems,
The Government looks on her station
For now, by the rules of the census report
It enters her—No Occupation.

          —Farmer's Advocate & Home Journal
           June 10, 1910

Summerfallowing on Bob Burk farm, Milo area, Alberta, 1917

III Rethinking The Role

The prairie was unequivocal in its message to pioneer women. "Be strong, be efficient, be competent; otherwise you and your family will not survive." Society was not so straightforward. It presented women with a number of conflicting demands.

One of the dictums of the early twentieth century was that women should not work outside the home. A real woman was a homebody who willingly cared for her children and mate as an act of love. She did not live in the vicious and uncertain public world where one had to fight to succeed. That was the man's lot: after all, he was smarter and more aggressive. The woman was emotional, conciliatory and tender. Her realm was the protected enclave of the home in which she acted not out of necessity but out of love and instinctual desire. In nurturing her family, a woman was to fulfill her biological and spiritual destiny. For her, serving other people was to be its own profound reward.

Thus, to be a "real woman" meant to be a contented wife, submissive, self-sacrificing, retiring, and resigned. If a woman thought she deserved more than the intangible rewards of affection, she was obviously unnatural. If she claimed to have ambitions other than homemaking and children, she was a mannish freak. If her husband treated her cruelly, she hadn't earned his love. It was not the model of reality which had failed: it was she.

Women were faced with enormous pressure to conform. The lesson of woman's lesser role was taught from the cradle on and reinforced by the clergy and the press. If a woman questioned this teaching, she was contradicting not only the laws of nature and everyday common sense, but ultimately God himself. Besides, there was the ambiguous evidence of her own experience. The majority of women *did* desire homes of their own; they did think of themselves as intuitive and sensitive; they did find joy in their children. Woman's role as homemaker and mother was undeniably central to the future of the economy and the nation. Was she not rearing the workers and citizens of tomorrow? Could a reasonable human being ask more from life than that?

From this perspective, what was happening to the pioneer woman was nothing more than the unfolding of her divinely ordained fate. The virtues of wifely servitude and motherly self-denial were the rationale for her continuing hard work. Many prairie women accepted the definition, but others had strong doubts. For a majority of farm women, life didn't seem to operate according to the "official" plan. Without such basic services as running water and medical care, their duties expanded almost beyond the limits of human endurance. Meanwhile, the "pay" had declined. Under frontier conditions, even a well-intentioned husband frequently could not provide the fatherly protection and financial support which society expected of him. The promised rewards of motherhood and kinship were often forfeited to isolation, child-bearing and overwork. Was this really all that a woman could expect of life?

There was occasionally evidence that the answer might be 'no'. The prairies were not, after all, culturally isolated from the rest of the world. By the early 1900's there were effective women's movements in Europe and the United States, and reports of their activities sometimes appeared in prairie papers. At the same time, the economies of the industrialized countries were undergoing change. While Western Canada remained predominantly rural, the Western world was becoming increasingly urban and industrial. As production shifted from the individual household to the factory, women were increasingly required in the labour force, and it gradually became more acceptable for women to work for pay. And as this happened, stories of successful career women became popular newspaper copy. Some of the coverage was antagonistic, but a few papers, notably the *Grain Growers' Guide*, were solidly supportive.

The new image of womanhood that emerged from the media was markedly different than the traditional idea of woman as wife. The "new woman" was an autonomous person, with rights and priorities of her own. She was intelligent, self-directing and financially independent, probably unmarried: a careerwoman. According to this perspective, women were not pre-ordained to wifehood; rather, they were socialized into it.

On the prairies, much of the debate about these ideas took place on the women's pages of weekly farm papers like the *Grain Growers' Guide, Farmers' Advocate, Norwest Farmer* and *The Western Producer,* and of urban dailies like the *Winnipeg Free Press, Regina Leader,* and *Calgary Albertan.* At a time when women's journalism was usually confined to kitchen hints and society gossip, prairie women were using newspapers as a way of coping with their own lives, their children, and their feelings about themselves. A few blunt realists began to raise difficult questions: Why must I humbly submit to recurring pregnancies when contraception is technically possible? Why does my husband own all the money and land, although we work together? Do my wishes and talents matter to no one but me? This remarkable openness is not only a reflection of the loneliness of pioneer life, but it is also a credit to the generosity and earnestness of the women who wrote and the editors who printed their letters.

An outstanding characteristic of the women's editors was their singular commitment to other women. Francis Marion Beynon, editor of "The Country Homemakers" page in the *Grain Growers' Guide* from 1912 to 1917, helped plan farm women's conventions, founded political equality leagues and master-minded petition campaigns. Both she and her sister Lillian Beynon Thomas ("Lillian Laurie" of the *Winnipeg Free Press*) were leaders of the women's suffrage movement in Manitoba. Violet McNaughton, for 25 years the editor of "Mainly for Women" in *The Western Producer*, was a Saskatchewan suffragist and first president of the Women Grain Growers' Association. These and other pioneer women journalists were, to use the phrase Francis Beynon applied to herself, "women's women". Together, they did much to foster a spirit of trust and sisterhood among country women and to encourage a critical re-examination of women's traditional role.

Many of the women who wrote to the papers were attracted to the image of the "new woman". All the same, an independent career was an unrealistic aspiration for most prairie women. Most women worked only while they awaited a chance to marry; as a result, the largest group of female wage earners was between 15 and 24 years old. Except for cases of extreme poverty, it was not acceptable for married women to work. In 1911, only 10 to 15 per cent of women over 10 years of age were employed for wages, with the lowest percentage in Saskatchewan and the highest in Manitoba. The vast majority of female wage-earners, married, widowed or single, took jobs not for the luxury of self-fulfillment, but in order to earn a living.

Since everyone knew that women were naturally intended to do housework, that is what most of them were hired to do. By far the majority of female wage-earners worked as maids in private homes, hotels and rooming houses. Non Anglo-Saxon immigrants were concentrated in these low-paying jobs. A woman experienced as a seamstress or milliner could take piece work into her home or, if she lived in the city, sew in the foul environment of a clothing factory. Here, the regulations governing working conditions and wages were rudimentary, and, where they existed at all, poorly enforced.

And so things continued until the outbreak of the first World War in August 1914. The first months of the war were marked by recession and serious unemployment among women workers. But as men left their jobs to go to the front, and as the economy felt the effects of wartime demand, the need for women's labour increased. The woman wage earner suddenly became "the girl behind the man behind the gun". No longer an isolated labourer struggling to keep herself alive in defiance of social conventions, she was now an essential part of the war effort. As women filled positions in industry, government and agriculture, they were publicly extolled for the very qualities which in peacetime they were expected to deny. In ads and editorials, the papers praised women for their productivity, competence and stamina in service of the nation. A permanent result of this wartime propaganda was the increase in public tolerance of women who worked for pay.

As soon as the war was over, the message to women was adjusted to suit the post-war needs of the economy. The first priority now was not convincing women of their strength, but finding jobs for the returned soldiers. Women were persistently reminded of their biological destiny and encouraged to return home. Some women were not persuaded, and remained in the occupations which had been opened for them by the War, particularly clerical work. But for the most part, women seem to have complied, because the percentage of prairie women described as gainfully employed was very nearly the same in 1921 as it had been 10 years before.

For most people on the prairies, "woman" still meant "wife". In spite of all the earnest debating about women's role and the effects of wartime career propaganda, marriage remained the dominant institution in most women's lives.

The girls are married far too young and are nearly always forced to marry against their own inclinations. Nearly all Galician girls are married between the ages of 13 and 16. After 16 they are considered old maids.

—School teacher's letter to Premier Martin
Saskatchewan, 1916

[When I came from the Ukraine to marry a man I didn't know]...the wedding was big...whole week—cook and eat and drink, but I go upstairs and cry because they are all strangers. I didn't know any people. There were Ukrainian people but I don't know any. I go upstairs and cry—for my village, for my brother and sister and my family.

—Mrs. Maksymuk
Edmonton, Alberta
Interview, 1974

Before my family went down to Saskatchewan, a young man was working for us and we got intimate with one another. We asked...permission to get married and my father said no. Well, the reason he didn't want us to go to get married was that he wanted me to go down there to Saskatchewan, you see. And my husband (of course he wasn't then my husband) didn't want me to go, so we went away and got married without my father's consent. We went away and got married, and came back and told them. Well, I was afraid I would get a spanking.

I was eighteen. And I was scared to go ask for my things—afraid I'd get a lickin' because my father was very strict and he used to hit, you see, or punish us. But my husband said, "Oh well, he can't do that now. You don't belong to him anymore." So finally, we got my box of things and went home to his house.

—Mrs. Beatrice Vincent (née Haskell)
Interview, 1975

The greatest insult came at the marriage ceremony when the minister asked "who giveth this woman," and some brother, or father or other man, unblushingly said he did, as though it were entirely a commercial transaction between men.

—Nellie McClung
Newspaper report, circa 1915

Wedding picture of
Mr. and Mrs. Maksymuk,
Edmonton

MARRIAGE IS SLAVERY

Dear Miss Beynon:

Never shall I kiss a despot, a small undertaker, a greedy master, who is keeping his wife, his comrade, the mother of his children just as the big undertakers their hired slaves—workers: a sweat shop (you call it home!); long hours of work, low wages, good enough to get food and some rags to cover the body. Right to the wealth you have produced with your hard work. All products of your work belong to the master you see! The women are in the same position in regard to the men as the workers to the masters. One difference: no modern master dares to hope that the workers who are toiling to produce wealth for their masters can love them. The big masters are frank; they say—give me your life, I'll give you some food and clothes to keep you alive with the sole purpose of forcing you to work and to raise children my future workers. Slaves! Such order (disorder?) is called the capitalist system. Under this system, while it lasts, there is not and cannot be any happy marriages, unless you call servility happiness.

The marriage of today does not mean love only. It is a partnership for business in the best case and slavery in the average case. How can a question of sincere affection and the money question, the business question be combined? How can sincere love be combined with the economical, social and political dependence? What is called love in the marriage of today is merely blunder, disguised mutual selfishness. Marrying, she hopes to get a protector and a home. He hopes to get an unpaid help and cheap pleasure in his home, where he is the master.

I am 53. I was married twice. My first husband was a university man. My second husband is a wage-slave, but for me there is very little difference. I do not speak about furniture, surroundings, I mean my personal, intimate spiritual life is just the same now as it was before. Economical dependence makes me suffer badly. I feel I am a "thing", not a human free being. There is enough to be unhappy even when your master is so good as my husband is good....I fight I never obey his will, I obey the rightness only. He respects in my person a self respecting human being and is sure that I will rather die than be a servant of the man who pretends to be my husband.

This is not my own opinion only, but the opinion of all our Russian intellectual women. I guess it should be the maxim of all women, but they have to educate themselves in this line.

...To educate, to teach the children to be free, noble people, we have to be not only mothers, but self respecting, high inspirited human beings, unless we want to raise wage-slaves and "cannon-fodder", or the meanest kind of people—masters.

Yours in the struggle for better times,

—*Mary Nicolaeff*
September 22, 1915
Grain Growers' Guide

Bridal party, Ponoka, Alberta, 1912

"I think of you always,"
   said HE.
"A little real PROOF would
   not hurt," said SHE.

"WIVES": PREACHER TELLS HOW THEY SHOULD ACT

An expectant audience filled Knox Church last night to hear Rev. Dr. Fulton preach on the subject of "Wives".

He quoted the Bible to show that wives' duty was to "love their husbands, to love their children, to be discreet, chaste, keepers of home, good, obedient to their husbands." He exhorted wives to retain their husbands' affections as it was said that "Love is a wife's only wages".

The question is: How is a wife to get her pay? A great number are not, he said. There are a good many homes where love is stark and dead, but the remedy is in the wife's hands. He advised her to make herself agreeable and attractive, keep herself neatly dressed, hair well in order, and always wear a smile. Keep the home cheerful, clean and cosy. Let her conversation be entertaining and manners pleasing as in the early days of marriage. The doctor elaborated on how the wife, for a short time after marriage, was always pleasing to her husband. She did not display her faults or bad temper and this made her more angelic in his eyes. Thus she gained his love.

—The Calgary Albertan
January 27, 1916

Life might take a snap at me any time. I thought of the prairie chickens off their guard, when they danced their mating dance; easy victims in their one mad delicious hour. Women were the same and for them life was as treacherous as ice. I had thought I was strong like Queen Elizabeth who kept clear of sex complications, but now I could see I was wavering. I knew that I would like to have a baby of my own sometime. I had resisted dolls all my life, not without a struggle. I had been scornful of the great trunk full of pillow shams and splashers and hem-stiched sheets that Lily Dewart had all ready. Marriage to me had a terrible finality about it. It seemed like the end of all ambition, and hope and aspiration. And yet I knew now since the baby had come that a child is greater than all books and all learning and that little first cry is mightier than the cheers of ten thousand people.

—*Nellie McClung*
Clearing In The West

Playing piano, Saskatchewan farm home

THE GIRL AND HER COLLEGE

All things being equal, a college training is...of inestimable value to a girl, as it is to a man, and she is the better equipped for her duties of wife and mother because of it....But in the majority of cases a college training is not feasible or possible. If going to college simply means to a girl's mind the fun to be had, it is infinitely better that she should remain at home. If a girl is inclined to be selfish and hungers simply for a brilliant career, it is wisest that the softening influence of a home remain her portion.

—The Calgary Herald
Circa 1900

There is no school better than the home for training girls for the womanly duties of life.

—Grain Growers' Guide
June, 1908

A GIRL AND HER EDUCATION

The educated girl of today is the well-trained pure thoughted girl—wholesome, refined, gentle, tender, radiating an atmosphere of brightness and purity and sympathetic strength. She is efficient in home making and in the uplifting power—humanity will be the better for her presence, the wiser for her counsel, the stronger for her sympathy. The world will be better, purer and brighter for her passing through it....

The well educated girl does not read printed poison, for she knows it weakens her brain power—her will power. She does not devour too many books. She realizes that what she reads largely determines her intellectual culture—the character of her education. She knows that the inspiration of a good book has made men great and women noble....She realizes that she has not come into the world to move through her life alone.

The educated girl is popular. She may not have a pretty face, but the reflection of her soul will make a charming face which lasts throughout her lifetime. "Take care of the first 20 years of your life and the next 20 years will take care of you!"

—*Pearl Richmond Hamilton*
The Western Home Monthly
January, 1916

Saskatchewan school girls

All my skill and effort went into our new home. My sister who lived in the United States, visited us that next summer. She was appalled with our living conditions. How could I be so stupid as to live in the bush? She was married, but had no family. She had stylish clothes, owned her own car, and possessed a license and diploma to operate her own barber shop. I couldn't help wishing I were her, and envied her for her possessions. Mother told me I had a diploma too, one of courage, faith, hope and tolerance.

—Mrs. Hoffman's Story
Pioneer Tales Of The Interlake

"A man well fed
On Home-made Bread
Will be proud of his wife
And love her"

We stayed at home. We could put our hair up when we were 18, 19 years old, before that we were only children with our hair down. When I finished school I wanted to go and train for a nurse. But girls didn't go out then and my father said "no". I was the only girl at that time and he thought that I should stay at home and learn to housekeep and help my mother....

—Margaret Collicut (née Murdock)
Edmonton, Alberta
Interview, 1967

"I knew nothing of business until my husband died," she said in her even voice, "I was a nice girl equipped for life, my poor mother thought. I could bake, sew, play the organ, and recite the 'Evening Hymn', and had made quilts, and a seed-wreath. But what good does that do me now, when I am the head of a house with five little children depending on me? I have to do a man's work, as well as a woman's, and in doing that I have found out a few things. Men are afraid of women, jealous of them, and unfair to them. They want women to be looking-glasses, howbeit false ones that make them look bigger than they are. Even my little boys want me to watch them when they are sleigh-riding down the hill.

"Especially strong in most men is their dislike of women, who know more than they do. I taught a hired man a new wrinkle about ploughing and he left me, he said he wasn't going to be bossed by a woman, and the neighbors thought he did exactly the right thing...They would do more for me if I were a helpless, pretty, little thing who would burst into tears...I cried plenty the first year I was left alone, and everyone was very kind to me then. Now, that I am really trying to run my farm and look after my family I meet plenty of opposition...But I can't keep on crying, even to get help. How I hate that song, 'Men must work and women must weep'. I can work like a man, I can plough, and run a binder...and believe me, my girls will get a man's education. They won't be left helplessly floundering like I was...."

—Nellie McClung
Clearing In The West

THE LANCERS

Children dancing, Calgary, 1899

Dear Editor:

Please allow me a little space to pass a few remarks on the speech given by Mrs. McClung recently.

In attempting to excuse the influx of women into public life, commercial and professional, she is putting up the many-times repeated statement "that the women are forced out of their homes on account of those industries which were once carried on in the homes now being done in our factories"....According to her theory, one would expect to see the girls working in the factories but instead of this they are seeking positions as stenographers...We also see women seeking to take up Law, Medicine, Politics, and growling because Theology will not admit them. Some of them want to be managers of stores, captains of ships, legislators, locomotive engineers, etc. Are they trying to limit their activities to those things which were once in the home? At the present time there are 400 women out of work in Winnipeg, saying nothing of the 5,000 men similarly situated, who appealed to the Women's Civil League (a suffragette organization) to see if they could not remedy matters. This League inquired into the matter and found that practically all of the girls could receive employment as domestics in good homes, but they were largely opposed to this....

This world always has had and always will have an intolerance for women who, with no moral right, attempt to defraud the privileges due to man and the same time the courtesies due to women. They must learn if they go into public life to take the bitter with the sweet....

I am, yours sincerely,
B.H.O. Harry

—The Independent Wawanesa
Methven, Manitoba
December 24, 1913

REVOLT OF WOMEN

A woman may leave a houseful of children behind her and go out all day, to a factory, to a washtub, to a sewing maching, to a scrubbing, to anybody's kitchen, to manual labor of whatever weight or physical excess; she may become idly giddy and spend seven days in the week at bridge or dance, at horserace or golf. Dr. Armstrong sees no loss to the State, to the children, to the "functions of womanhood", nor even to dear tender man. But let a handful of brainy women go out in the same way a few hours daily, to earn their living in chemistry, in modern languages, in electrical engineering, in mathematics, where the work is light, the hours short, the pay big, and behold, women are thwarting nature —they are behaving very unbecomingly and "are dragging men with them to destruction".

—*"Women's Sphere In Life And Labor"*
Grain Growers' Guide

Home economics class, Manitoba

Assinibioa, North West Territories

Dear M:

I am sorry you have to work so hard [as a domestic]. I have to work a great deal harder this summer than last of course. Mrs. Humphrys was not here last summer and that makes a great difference. She is never happy unless surrounded by visitors. There's very often people to luncheon, tea or dinner, not forgetting the dances. There were about 70 people here to a dance in July. They look like a lot of fools coming to be fed. I quite agree with you on the service question. I am tired of it myself and will quit it before long. I never was quite done up till this summer. The eldest daughter and myself in spring cleaning time colour washed all the house upstairs and down and painted all the wood work. It had never been done before. There's 13 rooms upstairs and 11 rooms down, beside a very large landing and hall. I really worked myself out till I was got quite weak. Of course I had the heavy part of it. Mrs. Humphrys bought a bottle of scott emulsion and gave me. I am thankful to say I am all right again now only much thinner than I used to be but none the worse for that.

Yours lovingly,
Martha

When a man goes out to farm labor he has regular hours for work. When a woman goes to farm labor, she works all the time, for no farmer will pay a woman wages unless he has work enough to keep her the long day, and paying work at that, such as butter-making, for her to do. Now, the quality of the labor or its profit or otherwise to the farmer ought not to govern the hours of labor for the domestic. She should not be compelled to work longer than the man. She should be allowed some waking hours of every day for recreation, for her own pursuits, whatever they may be. It is the confining and endless supervised long, drawn out working day that makes the lot of the average domestic intolerable. Since it is a necessity to work late in the evenings and early in the mornings on the farm, surely compensations could be worked in in the afternoons were the employers willing and humane.

—*Isobel*
"Around The Fireside"
Grain Growers' Guide

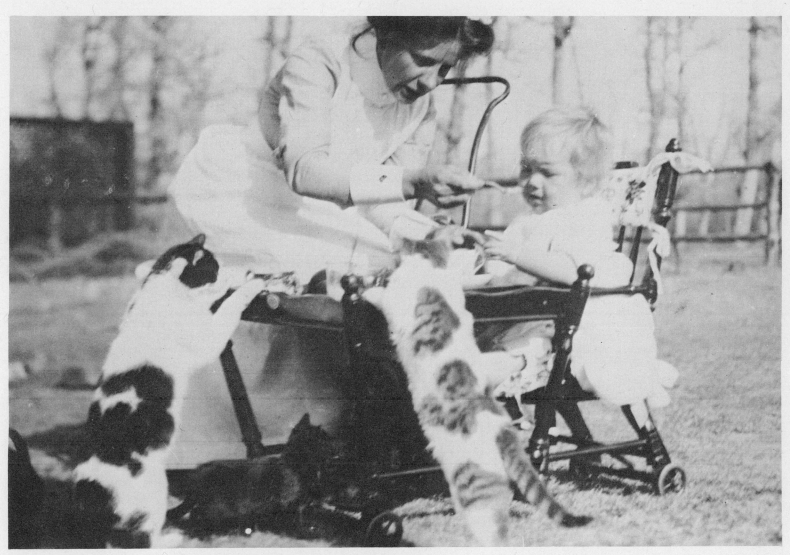

Nurse feeding baby, Bedingfeld Ranch, Pekisko, Alberta, 1912

BRILLIANT WESTERN WOMAN TALKS TO CANADIAN BUSINESS WOMEN'S CLUB

"Business is not a matter of sex, but of capacity," Mrs. Murphy said, and added: "That work is yours for which you are best adapted—even if it is to sing bass!"

With regard to the "equal-pay fallacy", she said that although in their war work woman had equalled man in efficiency, she got 50 to 85 percent less wages. Her present wage scale doesn't depend so much on her efficiency as on her employer.

The speaker quoted from a Toronto paper an item telling of a girl receiving $11 a week in a bank where she was "required to dress so that at all times she shall appear what she is not."

"I don't care who they are who give a girl $44 a month." Mrs. Murphy said, "they are profiteering in her blood and in her life and in her soul."

"It used to be considered an awful thing to send girls into offices, where there were supposed to be wicked employers and other dangers. But we have found out a wonderful thing. We have found out that this is not so. The most dangerous profession for women today is domestic service. Statistics in the United States, and they are probably much the same in Canada, show that eighty percent of the women who have gone wrong were in domestic service."

—Newspaper report
circa 1915

Domestics have been with the movement [of Ukrainians to Canada] since the beginning....Placement is still a problem with these girls...who are handicapped by their ignorance of English. We found evidence enough of this in a curb agent's office in Edmonton where twenty-five or thirty Ukrainian girls who were out of work came regularly for their mail. The Superintendent of the Employment Service Bureau of the city also said that: "The Ukrainian girls cannot be placed. Whereas German girls often speak English before they get here, none of the Ukrainians speak English."

All of which, taken along with the factors of a lower standard of living, lack of training, a flooded market for girls of this type, and inadequate supervision, may account for the fact that so many of them drift to the third-class restaurants of the cities. The proprietor of two or three Ukrainian newspapers referred on one occasion to the fact that Ukrainian girls might be found in most of the restaurants in the city [Winnipeg] . The unfortunate aspect of the situation is that not a few of the restaurants are places of questionable repute.

—Charles H. Young
The Ukrainian-Canadians

Prostitute

I started my own studio in 1920. I had the unfortunate position of being a woman. And in those days a woman in business was not recognized. I think I was the first woman west of Portage La Prairie to start a photographic studio of my own. And there were many, many times when I'd think I'd come to the end of my tether and just couldn't go on and then I'd be afraid. They'd say "I told you so." And I'd start in again.

—*Mrs. Gladys Reeves*
Edmonton, Alberta
Interview, 1966

One evening in 1886 my father surprised us all, as we sat at the tea-table, by telling mother that he had promised Mr. Davin to let me go to work at the "Leader Office" in Regina for a few weeks. He said that they were in need of more help in the folding and binding department. Mother was not very enthusiastic about it, but I was quite pleased with the idea, not only because it meant escape for a time from always distasteful housework, but also at the prospect of earning a little money to "help out".

Father said that the day's work began at 7:30 a.m. and ended at 6 p.m., with an hour off for dinner. My salary was to be $10.00 per month of 26 working days. This sounded like wealth to me and opened up vistas of new frocks and shoes all round; things which always seemed to be in short supply in the family. I was thirteen years old at this time, and as there was no young baby in the home now, could be spared more easily than usual. My mother said—so rightly—"Spared to go to school!" But I went into the "Leader Office" instead, and found it a school of sorts, and not by any means a bad one.

—*Mrs. Mary Davis*
"A Pinafored Printer"
Saskatchewan History

Dear Alberta West:

It seems to me that there is no difficulty in outlining a rosy prospect for an English family—well qualified to take care of themselves...If I were the "proficient housekeeper, poultry keeper, dairywoman and seamstress" of this family, I would immediately constitute myself the head of such a cosy home, and start a chicken farm. With eggs selling at 40 cents and 50 cents per dozen, I should attempt to make my fortune in this way....The typewriter could easily secure a good position at $600 or $700 per year in an office in town, and the teacher, after passing her examination could easily get a position in a public school. New rooms and schools being opened every month in the city, she could probably reside there all the time; if not she could get a very good position in some other part of the province and spend her holidays at home.

I am sure they would love it, the prairies are so magnificent! And with a pony of their own, they could have the best times imaginable in Calgary.

—*"Canadian Girl"*
Calgary, 1911

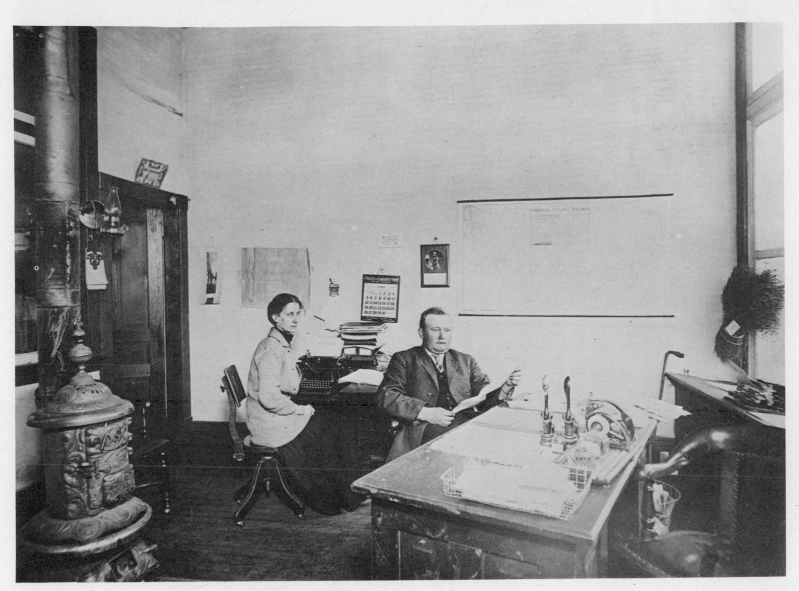

Real estate office in Three Hills, Alberta, 1914

When I started in Saskatoon [in 1928], my [fellow] teachers were...women in their late twenties...Many of them had come from Ontario or Nova Scotia, because...there'd been quite an influx of trained teachers who came from the East to fill the vacancies here in the West, because after all there weren't enough people growing up here to go into Normal School...I think most of my teachers were strong personalities, very devoted to their work...and good teachers, really top-notch.

—Caroline Robins
Past president, Saskatchewan Teachers' Federation
and Canadian Teachers' Federation

The teacher had a considerable influence...for good, not only among the children but among the older people also. It was said recently by a prominent Canadian writer that the real story of the country school teacher in Western Canada is one to which full justice has never yet been done, for it is a story that would tell of the struggles of one man, or one woman, who endeavours to handle the work of eight or nine grades single-handed; who has to direct and mould the characters, as well as the education, of children of many different nationalities, religions and types; who must conduct a fight, not only against the physical hardships occasioned by a climate of intense extremes of heat and cold, but often also against what has been termed "a measure of intellectual sparseness and social barrenness" little dreamed of by the average city dweller.

—Katherine Strange
With The West In Her Eyes

"Oh, that this too, too solid flesh would melt and thaw!" But it won't, and when I put my feet on the floor I can fancy that I hear them rattle...

This is one of those regulation little country schools with a row of ill-fitting windows up one side and down the other and a small square porch tacked on one corner. It is built with only a surface foundation and a floor guaranteed to admit, without question, all weather below zero.

The heating apparatus consists of a box stove for wood....It is too cold for the poor little children to sit at their desks, so the front seats have to be arranged around the stove....They arrive here cold from a two to four mile drive and come into a place that is like a barn for temperature and dingy and dirty into the bargain.

From a decorative point of view, the interior leaves much to be desired...Its lack of equipment is shocking....The only library is a small collection of Sunday school books relating impossible and insipid tales of...uninteresting youngsters.

Except the companionship of children of their own age there is not one feature of this school to appeal to children.

—Francis Beynon
Grain Growers' Guide
December 3, 1914

Sarcee Anglican School, Alberta, 1912

Dear Miss Dix:

I have a brother who earns a much bigger salary than I do. My mother is satisfied to have my brother pay her a fair board and have the rest of his money to spend as he pleases, but she makes me turn over my entire pay envelope to her and she gives me only back for my expenses what she thinks I should have. In a word, she considers that what my brother earns is his own, but what I earn belongs to her. When my brother comes home she thinks he should rest and she never asks him to do a thing about the house, but she demands that I help her get the dinner and wash the dishes afterward and help out with the sewing. Mother washes and mends my brother's clothes and keeps them looking tidy. I have to do my own. All of the girls that I work with have the same home conditions. Why do mothers treat their daughters so differently from their sons?

—Maud

Answer: Nobody knows, Maud. It is just the way mothers are built. A woman will offer her daughter up as a living sacrifice to the family...but she...calls upon the world to observe what a treasure heaven has blessed her with if her son does the smallest thing for her. Perhaps the reason that mothers are so much harder on their daughters is because the wage-earning girl is still so new that her mother has not yet had time to adjust herself to her. Perhaps, too deep for any one generation to eradicate it, there still lies the belief that a mother should control her daughter's expenditures. Mothers have not yet been able to see that when a girl becomes independent, her whole status in the household is changed and she should stand at least on an equal footing with her brothers.

Nor should a girl be expected to do housework after she has toiled all day. That is more than flesh and blood can stand. So many girls break down or fail to make good in business because they are worn out doing double duty....The great majority of mothers still think that daughters have no right to their pay envelopes and that sons have a right to theirs, and that their daughters should work both outside of the home and inside of it, while all that a boy should be expected to do is to enjoy himself after working hours.

And there you are, Maud. Brother will always be the fair-haired child with mother. She can't help it. It is biological.

—Dorothy Dix
The Calgary Albertan
October 14, 1929

The average wage of the 72,571 women wage-earners employed in the manufacturing industries in Canada in the year 1910 are shown by the Dominion census of manufacturers to have been 83 cents a day or $21.75 per month. These women are all over 16 years of age and many of them had children or parents to support. Upwards of 13,200 children under 16 years of age were also employed in the mills and factories of Canada in the same year and received 50 cents a day or $13.25 a month. The 376,872 men working for wages in our great manufacturing establishments received an average of $1.46 a day or $38.33 a month. While women work for $21.75 and men for $38.33 a month, in order that millionaires and multi-millionaires may be created it cannot be claimed that... protective tariffs protect the worker.

—Grain Growers' Guide
March 5, 1913

Clothing factory

WOMEN AND WAR

That the old theory that war makes for good times is a fallacy, and that instead it bears very heavily upon the home is being keenly felt already by the women of Canada....With the war has come also a financial panic, such as has not been known in years, resulting in the immediate discharge of hundreds of employees and a curtailment of the salaries of hundreds more. Here...women feel the pinch as keenly as the men. How to feed and clothe their families is the problem confronting scores of them in the homes where the bread winner has been given an unwelcome holiday. Some of them are going out and offering their services as wash and scrub women, but there is not, with the increasing financial stringency, an unlimited market for such labor. With a long cold winter facing them these women have every reason to be concerned for the future. Women are also feeling the effects of the war directly as competitors in the labor market. Partly owing to their recent invasion of the field of business and partly to the tacit understanding that marriage will, sooner or later, cause them to leave their work, the posts occupied by women are usually of a subordinate character, and it is in this quarter that the weeding out begins when the pressure of hard times is felt. Firms that employed six stenographers are managing with half that number or less; the department stores, where women employees are greatly in the majority, are weeding out the newcomers and incompetents; women are discharging their housemaids and doing their own work. As a result hundreds of women employees have found their means of livelihood in the business world suddenly stopped and themselves cut adrift at a season when there is not such a thing as a vacant position anywhere...

—Grain Growers' Guide
September 21, 1914

To the Women of Calgary:

Wives, mothers, daughters, sweethearts, I make this appeal to you. You have suffered, sacrificed, served. The blood of heroes and the tears of women have spiritual values. Your help and influence will not fail the empire in this hour of crisis. Our Dominion government wants 4,000 women to take the place of men in the munition and other factories of Canada. Women are wanted in Calgary and everywhere else in Canada to set free eligible men for overseas service. You have done much. You will do more. The war means more to you than all others. It means unspeakable anguish. It also means triumph. The enthronement of women side by side with men in every department of administration.

Women of Calgary, come to the great recruiting rally of women in the Orand theater, Thursday, June 29, at 3 p.m. National service, registration, and recruiting will be the topics.

G.W. Kerby
Major and Chief Recruiting Officer of the Province of Alberta

—The Calgary Albertan
June 24, 1916

Munitions factory
circa 1915

WOMEN'S VOLUNTEER RESERVE ORDERS

Monday, March 27—*Full parade at the drill hall, all those training for skirmishing display are requested to bring their rifles.*

Tuesday, March 28—*Target practice for sections 1, 2 and 3, at the range.*

Wednesday, March 29—*Ambulance class at the University at 7:45 p.m. Signalling class at the Alexandra block at 8 p.m.*

Thursday, March 30—*Target practice for sections 4, 5 and 6, at the range.*

Friday, March 31—*Full parade at the drill hall.*

—Margaret MacDonald, Captain and Adjutant

—Edmonton Journal
March 26, 1916

The call for which so many women have expressed a desire has come. The call for women soldiers. Not to fight in the treanches, but to do equally necessary work for the nation....It is true many women have not been trained. Specializing in women's vocations is a comparatively new idea. But one never knows what can be accomplished until the trail is made. Nothing is impossible to women with brains, ambition and a sense of humor. What can you do? As time goes on the nature of work to be handled will be varied. Can you do anything which would earn you bread and butter outside your own home? In the business world ability is the main factor. Personality, patience is a good asset. Women will now have to learn to leave undone the things whose accomplishment is not necessary, even if by so doing their fastidious souls are offended every hour of the day. They must do first the important thing, and after that attend to such details as their strength will permit and still leave them fitted for the big thing tomorrow.

—Edna Kells
Edmonton Journal
May 11, 1916

Edmonton Women, Colonel Craig Thinks, Can Easily Fill the Situations Occupied by Unmarried Men—Leave Men on the Farms, He Urges

"Let us hold a Woman's Civic day, for the purpose of demonstrating that a great majority of the work now done by young unmarried men could be done equally well by the women of the city. On that day the conductors on the street cars should be replaced by women, the taxis should be driven, and the stores clerked by them. In short, wherever possible, women should for that day take the places of the men..."

—Edmonton Journal
March 9, 1916

Decoration Day parade, 1916

When my son's regiment was mobilized and sent to the front I think that it never occurred to me, any more than it did to him, to question his duty....When, in those first few weeks of high patriotism his letters reported successful scouting or even devestating raids, I felt only a solemn satisfaction. But gradually through the months, when always more of the people's food supply and constantly more men were taken by the government for its military purposes, when I saw the state institutions for defectives closed, the schools abridged or dismissed, women and children put to work in factories under hours and conditions which had been legally prohibited years before, when the very governmental officials who had been so concerned for the welfare of the helpless were bent only upon the destruction of the enemy at whatever cost to their fellow citizens, the State itself gradually became for me an alien and hostile thing.

I am sure that I had reached these conclusions before my own tragedy came, before my son was fatally wounded in a scouting aeroplane and his body later thrown overboard in a lonely swamp. It was six weeks before I knew what had happened and it was during that period that I felt most strongly the folly and waste of putting men, trained as my son had been, to the barbaric system of killing.

—Mrs. Addams
Circa 1914-1916

Women have been discovered more or less since the war began. You know we always knew ourselves that we were here; we always knew that we had hands to work and brains to think and hearts to love; we always knew that we were a National asset but there were some people that had not just realized it yet, statesmen particularly....Now, in a peculiar way women have been discovered to be a war asset. Over in England where so many women are taking the places of men, even Mr. Asquith, who cannot be said to be an enthusiastic on the subject of women, admits that women are very valuable in time of war....

I like to think that woman's part in the war, in the work of the world, is not what she can do with her hands or what she can do in presiding over a mechanical machine; woman's part in the war, as I see it, is the same as woman's part in the world; it is to be that of a healer, a binder, a constructionist and not a destructionist.

I like the picture of the women in Red Cross work, making bandages, making comforts. Everywhere they are doing this work; it is typical; it is women's work; I like to think of that, that everyone of us, even though we are not in communication with the first line trenches, that we are in the back trenches trying to keep the home fires burning, to keep alive the fire and the warm glow of international friendship, trying to teach that internationalism which is greater than patriotism, trying to subjure that national patriotism which teaches us to love our own and hate every other. Beloved, that is the cause of all our trouble.

—Nellie McClung
Circa 1917

Clark's lumberyard, Edmonston, circa 1916

"Woman's sphere" was defined long ago, not by women, but by men; and the innate feeling that called on women to perpetuate the race kept them from rebelling against the decisions of the fathers of their children. But for the last decade women have been rebelling to some account and the rebels have often come into bad repute, but they surely prepared the way for the great change that is coming to the status of women.

The war, by taking away the men for other purposes, has thrown open nearly every class of work to women—and it will never be possible again to shift all women to one class—"Woman's sphere". It is a surprise to the women themselves that they come so readily to jobs for which they have had little or no training. It has been a wonderful thing for women, in that it has shown them that they have the ability to do other things than cook and scrub.

But this does not mean that the jobs of cooking, housekeeping and the raising of families will be no more; on the contrary, more women will do them willingly, for they will be recognized not as undesirable jobs...but as vocations, at which only the competent will be employed.These war times are teaching the woman the value of self-sufficiency, and self-esteem. She may find it necessary to help others by means of organizing helpful societies. It all develops her latent capacities.

—*Miriam Green Ellis*
Regina Leader
February 16, 1916

The Soldier: "Women are not entitled to vote. They cannot bear arms."
The Mother: "No, but we can bear armies."

Woman's work and woman's sphere have always furnished a favorite topic of conversation. Her activities and resourcefulness during the war exploded many of the privileges which for years she had claimed to be her right. Now that the war is over the public mind is seized with a new dread, and the subject for popular comment is whether woman will be willing to relinquish her new-found liberty and wider sphere of activity and resume her place as home-maker in the same old way, or will she continue to claim her present place in the industrial world and thus constitute one more of the already numerous after-the-war problems.

This, it is argued, would be a double tragedy, because she would turn her back upon home life and would at the same time keep out of employment vast numbers of men who would otherwise be needed in the various positions now occupied by women....We must admit that every woman has a right to choose the way in which she can best make her contribution to society, nor do we believe that we are running any risk by so doing, for the average woman will continue to feel that her contribution can best be made through the medium of the home...because, in the very nature of things, it is so, and the average woman instinctively loves home life.

—*Louise McKinney*
Canadian Home Journal
August, 1919

From the Annual Report of Neglected Children for the Province of Manitoba, 1912

IV Organizing For Reform

The effect of the first world war on woman's role was complex. Because much of women's work had always been done for nothing, the military crisis affected more than the relatively small group of women who were working for wages. Most women put their energy into volunteer labour. Throughout Canada, from the largest city to the most insignificant town, groups of women met regularly to roll bandages, package "soldiers' comforts" and knit socks for "the boys". Whether it was as off-duty factory workers organizing day care centres or as service club members doing patriotic chores, the war brought women together.

To be more accurate, the war accelerated a process which had been introduced to the prairies about two decades before. The late nineteenth and early twentieth centuries saw the formation of a number of women's organizations in the East, several of which moved west with the settlers. The Canadian chapter of the Women's Christian Temperance Union began organizing in Ontario around 1875 and spread to the prairies in 1886. The National Council of Women, initiated in Ottawa by Lady Ishbel Aberdeen, had branches in major prairie cities after 1895. By the 1920's, there were so many different associations that a person with leisure could rise to national prominence as a professional volunteer or "club woman", as she would then have been called. Middle class women sometimes joked that they were "clubbed" to death!

Because there were so many organizations, each representing a special interest group, the club movement did little to soften the differences of class and opinion which divided women socially. In the city, for example, the well-to-do ladies of the Local Council of Women might not see eye to eye with the Women's Labour League. The Methodist Women's Missionary Society would seldom cooperate with the Presbyterian Ladies Aid or the Catholic Women's Auxiliary. The Women's Canadian Club, with its dedication to British-Canadian culture and loyalty to the Queen, was not always friendly to ethnic organizations which were fiercely determined not to conform. There were associations for imperialists, pacifists, labourers, and professionals. In fact, there seemed to be a club for every class and cause.

Even in rural communities, women were often divided by politics, religion and language. One of the very few organizations which admitted any woman with no questions asked was the Women's Institute. The concept of government-sponsored clubs for isolated rural women was developed by Adelaide Hoodless of Ontario around the turn of the century. By 1910, Women's Institutes had been organized in all three prairie provinces, where lonely rural women, eager for a chance to get together and learn from one another, responded with real enthusiasm. The aim of the movement was to educate women as homemakers and to inspire them with the dignity and significance of their profession. Because of the government sponsorship, Institutes were discouraged from becoming involved with controversial issues such as women's suffrage.

By 1914, there was a second network of farm women's groups in Alberta and Saskatchewan with overtly political aims. The United Farm Women of Alberta and the Women Grain Growers' Association of Saskatchewan were the women's section of the farm protest movement. (Women in Manitoba did not organize along these lines until 1918.) Although they were closely affiliated with "men's" organizations, neither the UFWA nor the WGGA thought of itself as a women's auxiliary. Instead, they saw themselves as co-combatants in the struggle against the political, economic and social enemies of prairie agriculture. They were members in full standing of the farm movement who preferred working together as women, from a woman's point of view.

Because of their political stance, the UFWA and WGGA didn't attract the same breadth of membership as the Women's Institutes. To feel at home in the former, one had to embrace not only the "radical" perspective of the farmers' movement, but some unconventional ideas about the place of women in society. For many women, the Institutes, with their emphasis on the social importance of women's work in the home, were feminist enough. These women could not agree with the farm movement that women had a right and a duty to participate directly in public affairs. The Institutes were alliances of wives and mothers committed to upgrading society by strengthening the home. The United Farm Women and Women Grain Growers thought of themselves less as wives than as partners. Their preference was to upgrade home life by reforming the economic and legal framework of society.

This subtle difference in philosophy had some effect on the activities and tactics of the organizations. While the Institutes usually confined their discussion to homemaking and their service work to their own communities, the farm movement women delved into politics, economics and province-wide reforms. All the same, there was a considerable community of interests between the two groups: philosophy aside, a woman was still a woman, somebody interested in children, health care, education, and other people's well-being.

Responsible motherhood was a theme common to both branches of the rural women's movement. In "conservative" circles, the home was recognized as a component of the State; hence, homemakers were seen as nation-builders, with all the responsibility that entailed. Among change-oriented women, motherhood took on a more political cast. This latter group responded to arguments like the one made by Francis Beynon of the *Grain Growers'*

Guide in a 1913 editorial:

> We have too long been contented with the kind of motherhood that can look out of the window and see little children toiling incredible hours in factories and canning sheds over the way...and say calmly, "Thank God, it isn't my children", or who can see the poor wayward girl driven into a life of disgrace and shame by economic conditions and turn coolly away, content that her daughter is chaste; with the sort of motherhood that can know that in poor districts of our cities tiny babies are dying like flies and yet feel no responsibility for the conditions that cause their death.
>
> I tell you, sisters, this kind of motherhood isn't good enough for the present day. We want a new spirit of motherhood, mothers whose love for their own children teaches them love for all children; mothers who will not boast of their weakness but seek for strength to fight the battle for their own and their neighbour's children.

Volunteer womanpower pioneered many of the community services now provided by the state. In the course of mothering their communities, both farm and city women established services like libraries, hospitals, homes for the disabled, schools for retarded children, and hostels for unwed mothers. The transition of rural hospitals and public health clinics to government funding is also credited to prairie women's organizations, specifically to the United Farm Women of Alberta and the Women Grain Growers' Association.

The success of women's organizations in achieving this kind of reform was sometimes taken as evidence of the humanizing contribution that women might make to society if they were given an equal chance. Those who found this idea inspiring also thought it telling that the work of nurturing had been left to women. It seemed just another unwelcome demonstration of the low value that society placed on women, on feminine values, and even on the quality of human life.

In the old days when a woman's hours were from 5 a.m. to 5 a.m., we did not hear much talk of discontent among women, because they had not time to even talk, and certainly could not get together. The horse on the treadmill may be very discontented, but he is not disposed to tell his troubles, for he cannot stop to talk.

It is the women, who now have leisure, who are doing the talking. For generations, women have been thinking, and thought without expression is dynamic and gathers volume by repression. Evolution when blocked and suppressed becomes revolution.

—Nellie McClung
In Times Like These

REVOLT OF WOMEN

The State-made economic conditions of today (which conditions woman has no voice in) allow woman a husband it is true, but they do not make it possible for that husband to provide a comfortable time for her, and a proper rearing for her children; and in order to acquire the decencies of life for them, the woman becomes a "bounden" slave, and is compelled to crucify herself daily to their needs. The average mother has no past, no present, no future. Her personal identity is lost in a clamor for bread.

—Grain Growers' Guide
Circa 1914

Farm woman, Didsbury, Alberta, circa 1920

WOMEN NEED TO GET OUT

I had become so used to not going any place that I never thought of doing so, just stopped at home and kept at the everlasting work, which some way never seemed to get less, until with overwork and the eternal monotony my health gave way and I was a complete wreck. Then I began to realize how narrow the last two years of my life had been since moving from the homestead. I did not know my neighbour women who only lived two miles from me, and how I wished in my illness for a kind friend. I did not blame my neighbours as I knew I was as much to blame as they and that we were all making a big mistake. In looking through the Grain Growers' Guide I read where the women of Saskatchewan were forming a W.G.G.A. (Women Grain Growers' Association). I was quite taken with the idea and thought that we should do likewise. I asked my husband to go with me to the home of a neighbour, whom I had never seen. The result was that we now have a Women's Section of the G.G.A. with twenty-five paid up members.

I find my work does not suffer when I take half a day off to attend our meeting or visit a neighbour, and whereas my doctor's bills used to be from fifty to one hundred dollars per year, in the last year since I have taken up other interests outside my home, I have not had one dollar of a doctor's fee. I might say my worst troubles were bad nerves and a weak heart.

—*"Hope"*,
Grain Growers' Guide
April 21, 1915

Women's organizations...have come into being, as an expression of women's inherent desire to make life easier for someone, and the world a better place to live in. When the pioneer woman hurried through her own work, and then walked across the snowy field, with three loaves of bread, and her last jar of preserves, to minister to her sick neighbour and stayed to clean the house, wash the children, and cook a meal, she laid the foundation for the Victorian Order of Nurses, and the Women's Institutes. When she went over to the school to hearten the teacher, who was young and homesick, and talked over with her the problem of the Zink family whose big boy Bill would neither work in school nor let any one else work, she was laying the corner stone of her great parent-teachers association. And when she gathered two other neighbour women and together they pieced a quilt for the new preacher's rapidly increasing family, she became the forerunner of the great and powerful Ladies Aid and Missionary Societies whose splendid activities each year would fill many volumes.

—*Nellie McClung*
Manuscript, personal papers

Saskatchewan women

We belonged to the United Farm Women's Group....We done a lot of nice things. Lots of times when there were families, sometimes there were widows and sometimes there were widowers left with children, and we used to go and make clothes and do things for them. And also give them food. Lots of them didn't have much to eat.

—*Mrs. Mossen, midwife*
Edmonton, Alberta
Interview, 1974

Now a lot of the war brides that came out after the First War had never been on a farm. They didn't know the first thing about making butter, or making bread. Well, somebody would show them. They'd have a demonstration. They'd make bread or butter at the meeting—and then these women would say "Well, I'll try that"—and gradually got to learn how to do these things—and took a pride in doing it. Of course, a lot of those English women—they could do all sorts of needlework, better than some of our other people could and they just sort of traded information.

—*Mrs. Rogers*
Past president, Alberta Women's Institute
Interview, 1974

A women's gathering

The answer given by local organizations to the question "What are the chief difficulties you find in carrying on the work successfully " was "Babies". One Club reports that half their membership have babies under three years old, while the secretary herself has two under that age.... And that brings us face to face with a problem that perplexes every conscientious, but intelligent and public-spirited mother. It is your problem and mine—namely, under what conditions are we justified in confining our attention to our homes to the exclusion of all matters of public interest...

—United Farm Women of Alberta,
Annual Report, 1917

The women bring their babies to the meetings...and that means they are determined to come. Women themselves are largely to blame for conditions. They are too much inclined to suffer in silence. They will not speak up on their own behalf and develop a martyr complex which is hard to break, but I can get closer to them than a stranger, for they know that I know what I'm talking about for I, too, have travelled the cold road and had my hair frozen to the bed clothes at night.

—Nellie McClung
The Stream Runs Fast

Well, the need was mainly isolation—a place to get together, a place where you could meet people—that had the same interests as you had. You must remember that when the Institute started, out here, the people were scattered. Many of them wouldn't see anybody for a week—or longer—and some of them just couldn't take it. That's why so many of them ended up in Ponoka [mental hospital]—just the loneliness. If they had children, it wasn't so bad, but if anybody went to town father went to town....On the other hand, the Institute would never have got very far if it hadn't been for the cooperation of the men...We have pictures of a wagon full of women, all gathered up and being brought in—and it was no "hour meeting"—it was an afternoon. And, you brought the children...somebody would take them outside or in another room and entertain them. So, the youngsters liked it too. You might have a Ukrainian here. You might have a Scandinavian here. You might have an American over there—and you didn't have much in common—and the thing was to get a common ground. But of course if they had children—that was a common ground—the care and feeding of children. That was the original start of the Institute.

—Mrs. Rogers
Past president of Alberta Women's Institute
Interview, 1974

Meeting of the Women's Christian Temperance Union, Rama, Saskatchewan, 1913

TOO MUCH KITCHEN

What do you think about this [Women's Institute] program? Is it not merely a program for very young schoolgirls? Does this program speak to your heart and intellect? Does this program give us a larger field than the usual "women's yard"? Always suggestions about housework, knitting, and the main woman's destination: "preparing of dainty side-dishes and salads". Kitchen, kitchen, and again kitchen!

—Mary Nicolaeff
  Grain Growers' Guide,
  September 16, 1915

[Reply to Mary Nicolaeff]

All great changes require much time and instead of being peeved about the domestic character of the program...I think you might find cause for thanksgiving in the fact that in the very first year of their existence they are studying parliamentary procedure, the history of their great women, and social settlement work in great cities.

Be patient with these women's clubs my friend, and you will see them grow into something better than either you or I could foretell.

—Francis Marion Beynon
  Grain Growers' Guide,
  September 16, 1915

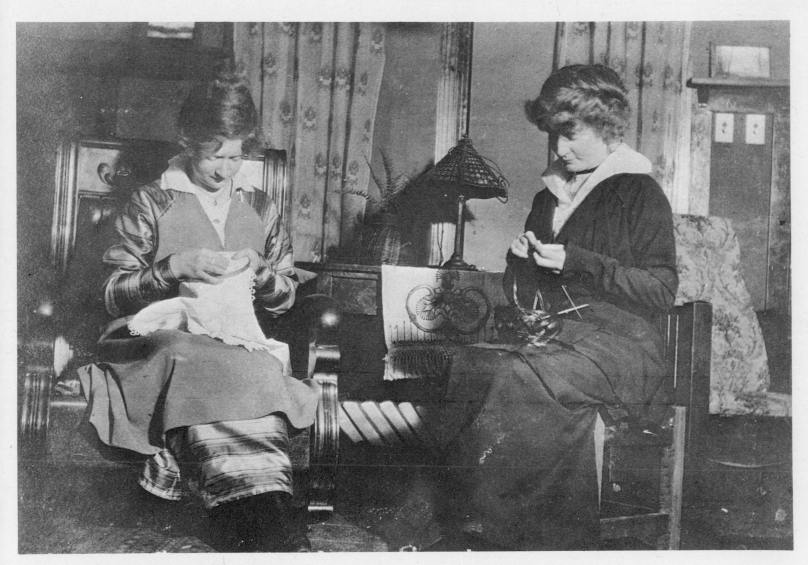

Embroidering and crocheting, 1912

I must pay my tribute to the brave women of the W.C.T.U. Looking back at our life in the small town I see we owed much to the activities of the W.C.T.U. and these initials, I hasten to explain, stand for "Women's Christian Temperance Union", and not "Women Continually Torment Us", as some have believed. They have what they called the do-everything policy. And good work helping for a neighbour, the education of a child. If any woman has a desire to help, in any way, the W.C.T.U. has a place for her.

It was the W.C.T.U. who planned debates, and spelling matches, and ran a reading room, wherein the Review of Reviews, and Scribners and McClure's magazines could be read, along with the *Family Herald,* the *Witness* and others.

We could have coffee sent up to us in honest, thick, white cups from the restaurant below, at two cups for five cents, just to give the conversation a continental flavour, and as we argued on annexation with the United States or the relative value of science or literature in the schools, or whether or not it is possible to live without sin, we felt that we were living in the best tradition of the coffee houses of London.

They were a resolute band of women, these early Crusaders, and I am always glad I met them and fell under their influence at an early age. A composite picture of the leaders at that time would show a tall, thin woman with her hair parted in the middle and waved back into a bun at the back of her well-shaped head, a crisp white frill at her neck fastened with a cameo brooch, a hunting case watch pinned on her left shoulder, secured by a gold chain around her neck; black henrietta cloth dress, black stockings, and a white handkerchief, a white bow ribbon, probably tied on the watch chain; clear eye, a light hand with cakes, and not afraid of anything!

—*Nellie McClung*
The Stream Runs Fast

Hillhurst Presbyterian Sunday School group, circa 1912

I enjoyed my association with the Canadian Women's Press Club...There great problems were discussed and the seed germ of the suffrage association was planted. The immediate cause of our desire to organize was the plight of women workers in small factories. Some of our members had visited these and we were greatly stirred over the question of long hours, small wages and distressing working conditions.

Mrs. Claude Nash...and I were deputed to bring pressure to bear on the government for the appointment of a woman factory inspector. We decided to go to see Sir Rodmond Roblin, the Premier, and if possible, get him to come with us to see some of the factories. We conducted the Premier down dark, slippery stairs to an airless basement where light in mid-day came from gaunt light bulbs, hanging from smoky ceilings. The floor was littered with refuse of apple peelings and discarded clothing. There was no ventilation and no heat. The room was full of untidy women, operating sewing machines and equally unattractive men cutting out garments on long tables...We led the Premier through a side door into the foul passage where a queue had formed before a door marked "Toilet". We could see that Sir Rodmond was deeply shocked that we should know about such things but Mrs. Nash led the way, and I pushed him along from behind. We drew his attention to the fact that there was no separate accommodation for the women, and we did not need to mention that the plumbing had evidently gone wrong. We knew that he was soon going to bolt away from us, so we didn't spare him anything.

"For God's sake, let me out of here," he cried at last. "I'm choking! I never knew such hell holes existed!"

"These people work from 8:30 to 6:00, Sir Rodmond. Six days a week," Mrs. Nash told him sweetly. "But no doubt they get used to it." I am afraid her sarcasm was lost on Sir Rodmond. With this understanding we parted, thanking Sir Rodmond for giving us so much of his time.

Our investigations went on. We were only amateurs but we did find out a few things about how the "other half" lived. We made some other discoveries too. We found out that the Local Council of Women could not be our medium. There were too many women in it who were afraid to be associated with any controversial subject. Their husbands would not let them "go active". It might imperil their jobs. The long tentacles of the political octopus reached far. So one night at Jane Hample's house on Wolseley Avenue we organized the *Political Equality League,* with a membership of about fifteen. We believed that fifteen good women who were not afraid to challenge public opinion could lay the foundations better than a thousand. Some good work had been already done by the Icelandic women of the city, who had organized the first suffrage society many years before, and the W.C.T.U. women could always be counted on and the same was true of the Labor women.

—*Nellie McClung*
The Stream Runs Fast

Canadian Women's Press Club room, Winnipeg, circa 1912

Women have dispensed charity for many, many years, but gradually it has dawned upon them that the most of our charity is very ineffectual and only smoothes things over, without ever striking the root....

A woman may warn factory girls against sin, but if she urges more sanitary surroundings, she finds herself in that realm of politics, confronted by a factory act on which no profane female hand must be laid.

—Nellie McClung
Newspaper report
May 9, 1916

I attended the convention of Women's Institutes in Edmonton and had a *very* pleasant time. It was well done, good music, all the big-wigs, and Gov. to help, and very, very different to our own higgledy-piggledy affair in Calgary, but their line of work to tell you the truth does not interest me very much—there is too much of the housekeeping business about it, and for my part I think the farm women want to be taken out of their housekeeping troubles, and made to realize there are other things of interest in the world, and that they do their housekeeping all the better for thinking of outside affairs.

—Irene Parlby
Letter to Violet McNaughton
March 14, 1916

The rural women of Alberta were the white hope of the progressive movement in that province. The Women's Institutes and United Farm Women were not afraid to tackle social problems and their reading courses and discussions showed serious purpose. The women of the cities were more likely to be entangled in social affairs and in danger of wasting their time in matters of constitution and procedure, such as "Who should sit at the head table at their annual banquet?" but there was real stuff in the countrywomen.

—Nellie McClung
The Stream Runs Fast

Wide-awake women realized that back of their special problems—the efficient management of the home, and the training and care of children—lay the economic problem. Labor-saving devices, conservation of health, better rural schools and higher education were directly connected with better markets, co-operative buying and selling, and better agricultural credit. In other words, the farmer's problem was his wife's problem also. What could be more logical than for her to assist the farmers' movement? And that is exactly what happened.

—"Working Hints for Local Unions of The United Farm Women of Alberta"
U.F.W.A. pamphlet

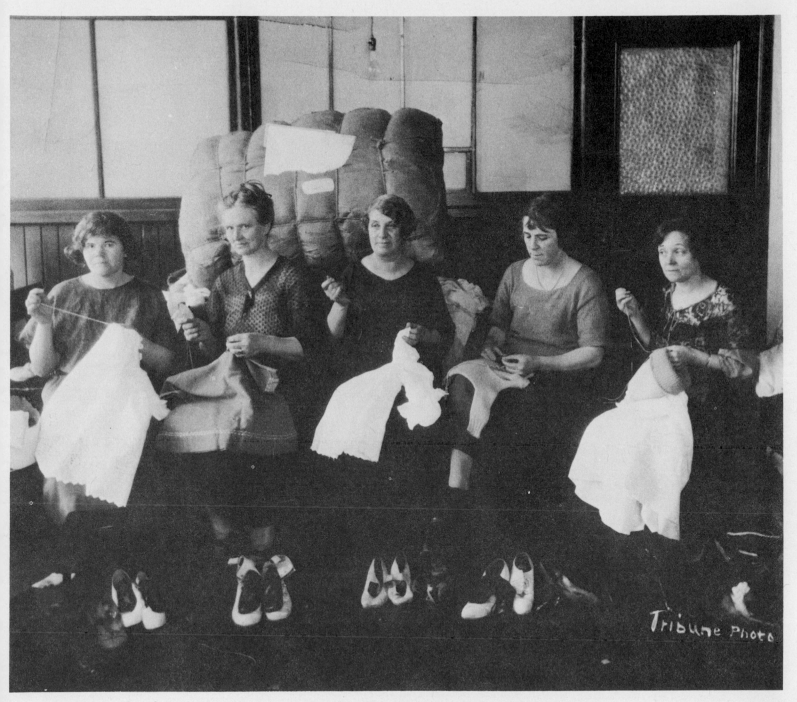

Women's Labor League preparing relief bundles for Nova Scotia coal miners, circa 1925

Picture our absurd nervousness [at the early U.F.W.A. convention] when we rose to give our reports or offer suggestions. Where was the courage of the Pioneer? We were scared to open our mouths; afraid to frame or move a resolution! Shaking knees! Trembling voices!...

We were groping blindly at those first meetings, toward a vision but dimly discerned; a vision which was to be made clear to us as the years went on.

I was elected first President, with the gigantic and rather terrifying task of building up a Provincial organization, of evolving policies and fixing a goal toward which to work. We had no money to work with, no prestige, and were to co-operate with a men's group which, while outwardly polite, did not at first realize the added strength which the women would lend to their own movement.

—*Irene Parlby*
"A While Ago and Today"
Canadian Magazine
July, 1928

Not a few have asked me what will be the best thing to come out of the union of men and women in the Grain Growers' Associations. Unhesitatingly I would say "comradeship". The working together for common objects without the eternal intrusion of the feminine and masculine. In other words they will more and more remember they are human beings and the emphasis on sex will be less, to the mutual advantage of both. Sometimes in the not too distant years they will call each other "men and women" and the man in the chair will cease to say "you men" and "now men" let us do so and so and in the next breath "the ladies". These be small things you say. Granted, but straws show the direction of the wind.

—*E.Cora Hind*
The Western Home Monthly
March, 1915

First executive of the United Farm Women of Alberta; Irene Parlby (bottom row, third from right)

I live in a fairly well-settled part of the country and we have no less than five towns within a radius of twenty miles. In all these towns, there is but one doctor, and needless to say, at times he is kept going night and day. We are almost as badly off for nurses, and I have known several cases within the past two years, in close proximity, where children have been born into the world without either doctor or nurse being present. Now, what I want to know is, can we women not do something to try to remedy this state of affairs. The government is willing to advance money to help us build elevators and save us from being robbed by the big grain combines, are they not first as willing to advance some, to try and get a large number of competent nurses and midwives from some of the older settled countries, to come in and save a lot of anxiety and suffering which hosts of expectant mothers are experiencing all year round, in all the newer settled parts of her Prairie Provinces.

—*Another Englishwoman*
Grain Growers' Guide
March 5, 1913

Women of the town had organized to help house and feed a large group of immigrants arriving by train. A number of Russians and Galacians were found to be suffering from pneumonia and had to be separated from the others and nursed; some of them died. The dreadful experience of having no place to take these sick folk so impressed the women of Portage that they determined to start an agitation for a hospital. They approached first the doctors who were very sympathetic but could give little hope of raising enough money. It was to the business men that the women appealed for money. They were very pessimistic about raising enough money....The women, nothing daunted, started on a money raising campaign. They gave parties, concerts and bazaars and finally had enough money for a beginning. They reconstructed the old city hall and finally opened with a staff of one trained nurse, 2 student nurses and 10 beds.

—*Mrs. Stidston*
Archives interview

Organized farm women...did a lot of things that should have been done by someone else. For instance...the people at Sexsmith wanted a municipal hospital—but the municipalities voted it down. Well, the Institute...raised enough money to start, and they built a cottage hospital at Sexsmith. And after it was a going concern, then the municipality said "Oh, that's a fine idea." They took it over as if it was their idea from the start. You see, they wouldn't credit it to the women. And down at Tofield...they couldn't afford a library there. Well, the women...started a library, until they had several thousand books, and it was a real going concern..."Oh, that was fine. That's ours." It became the town library. That happened again and again. The Institute started something and then it was taken over by the people who should have done it in the first place.

Prairie Circle Ladies' Group, Cereal, Alberta, circa 1916

Now when...the women came in from the north, they wanted this little hospital. The Minister said "Well, we'll discuss it. We'll think about it." "Well," the women said, "while you discuss it, our women die!" They weren't making any bones about it all. They *knew* the need.

—*Mrs. Rogers*
Past president of the Alberta Women's Institute
Interview, 1974

Because the care of the race is not the man's job, it has never appealed to him in its full significance. It has ever taken a secondary place. For this reason, medical inspection of our rural school children, rural hospitals, rural nurses, are still things we see only in our dreams. It is up to you, as organised women, to take up your burden, to shoulder your work, part of your work which was taken out of the home in the dim past of history, and bring these dreams to life. Perhaps we must not look too much for the help of the men in this movement. The bearing of the race, and the care of the race is the woman's job.

—United Farm Women Annual Report
1917

A prevailing spirit seems to be that "we are our sisters' keepers", and we are not doing our duty to others when remaining apathetic to affairs that are constantly calling for a change for the better.

—*Erma Stocking*
Secretary, Women Grain Growers' Association
Grain Growers' Guide *1914*

Prairie sisterhood

V Changing The Law

CANADA NEEDS A "CLEAN-UP" WEEK

Whatever their political and philosophical leanings, many of the women's clubs did similar kinds of work. In public affairs, as in private life, women concentrated on "welfare", while men were concerned with "wealth". Regardless of their membership or specific objectives, women's organizations generally took interest in causes like temperance, child welfare, education, public health and women's rights. Two of the legal reforms which aroused widespread concern among public-minded women were guardianship laws and married women's property rights.

Western Canadian mothers did not become legal parents until after World War I. Before that time, a father was empowered to manage his children's property, collect their income and determine their religion and education. Without consulting the mother, he could appoint a guardian in his lifetime or by will. He might even unilaterally put the children up for adoption. If he thought his wife an unfit mother, he could bar her from seeing them. A woman's only recourse was through the courts: at the judge's discretion, she might be granted custody or guaranteed access to her family in spite of the father's wishes. But this was to happen only in exceptional cases. The law made it clear that under ordinary circumstances, the father was to be the sole and unchallenged parent.

The other side of the coin, of course, was that the father was legally responsible for his family's support. The only case in which this arrangement did not apply was illegitimacy. An unmarried mother bore all parental responsibility until 1912 in Manitoba and Saskatchewan, and 1923 in Alberta. In those years, acts were passed requiring the father of an illegitimate child to contribute to its support, if filiation could be established. It was a big "if": the mother's testimony was not sufficient for conviction, and corroborating evidence was hard to get.

No one seems to have suggested government relief for unwed mothers. Governments of the period were committed to the stern virtues of personal responsibility. Why should the sober, industrious citizen encourage rampant parental irresponsibility? In 1916, the Manitoba government did begin to provide mothers' allowances to poor women, but only if their husbands were dead or clearly incapable of supporting the children. (Alberta and Saskatchewan passed similar legislation in 1922.) The object of the legislation was to free the mother from wage labour so she could care for her family at home. If the father were theoretically capable of paying the bills—even if he obviously had no intention of doing so—the State was unwilling to intervene. A man might beat his wife until she left him, or simply abandon her, but he was still legally responsible for his family's support. The wife could apply to the courts for a maintenance order, and do her best to collect, but in the end, the burden fell to her by default.

At a time when unskilled women wage-earners were generally restricted to domestic labour, this must have been a crushing responsibility. It was not made any lighter by property laws which denied married women any return for their work as wives. The inequities were particularly galling for the woman on the farm. Unlike the United States, Canada did not open homesteads to wives or single women. Only if she were the head of a household could a woman, like any male over eighteen, earn title to a quarter section of land by farming it. A wife or daughter might toil alongside her menfolk, contributing equally to the fulfillment of the homestead requirements, but in the end, the men owned the land. "Dower", a wife's traditional claim to a share of her husband's estate, had been suspended in Manitoba since 1885, and elsewhere in the West since 1887.

Obviously, these regulations thwarted the few women who wanted farms of their own. They hampered families with daughters that could not enlarge their farms as cheaply as those with sons eligible for homesteads. But most significantly, they hurt married women. Almost all of the land in western Canada, hence almost all the income, was legally owned and controlled by men. Individual couples were permitted to register joint ownership of their property, but few did so. It took an unusually generous and secure man to grant his wife that kind of concrete equality at a time when it was not customary. In fact, some men reportedly went to the other extreme and refused their wives any share of farm lands or income, even by inheritance.

The regulations which disqualified women from filing for homesteads were not changed, in spite of a flurry of protest from readers of the *Grain Growers' Guide* around 1910. Married women's property rights were improved, but not without a fight. In Alberta and Saskatchewan, the changes came in two stages: one guaranteed that a wife would receive a piece of her husband's estate, and the other enabled her to prevent a transaction involving her home. The first progress is generally credited to Emily Murphy, who wrangled with Alberta legislators over the provisions of that province's Married Women's Relief Act of 1910. In its final form, this act authorized a judge to overrule a man's will if he left his wife an inadequate inheritance, but it did not fix a minimum bequest. That was left to the Intestate Succession Act of 1920 which set aside a third of one spouse's holdings for the other if they had children, and the entire estate if they were childless. The Saskatchewan Devolution of Estates Act of 1919 had the same provisions.

Stage two came in the Saskatchewan Homestead Act and the Alberta Married Women's Home Protection Act, both passed in 1915. Under this legislation, a husband was forbidden to sell, mortgage, transfer or bequest the family home or the land on which it stood without the wife's written consent. In Manitoba, both these provisions (the guaranteed inheritance and the wife's right of veto) were written into one law, the Dower Act of 1918.

Put simply, these laws tried to assure that a woman could be left neither homeless nor disinherited. Although there were loopholes, the acts did provide some measure of protection for women in drastically unsuccessful marriages. But they stopped far short of the real security which might have been offered by recognition of the economic value of women's work. What women needed was not just a veto of transactions involving their homes, but ownership of property acquired during marriage in addition to a guaranteed inheritance after their husbands' deaths. They could have used a claim on the year-by-year income which they had helped to earn. The law offered to women as charity what should have come to them by right.

It is quite true that women have been the world's dependents. They have been the unpaid servants of men. What they received of the good things of life they have come by some man's bounty. Their claim is on the grounds of compassion.

—*Nellie McClung*
Manuscript, personal papers

There is no harder worked woman than the woman on the farm. Not only must she perform her duties as housewife, not only must she nurse and care for her children, but she is expected to be, and usually is the general servant of the farm itself. Her working day is the length of time she can manage to stand upon her legs. Her reward is desertion by her children when they are old enough to take care of themselves. Poverty and isolation make her function of mother-hood a real hardship and burden, and self-neglect makes her old before her years.

—The Western Producer
October 23, 1924

I know two women myself who do as much work out-doors as any three men. These women have horses and cattle of their own and work the land them-selves; but they have to rent it. They cannot yet afford to buy it and the law forbids them to homestead and so they have to pay rent. They have not got an even chance with men and yet we always call them the "weaker sex". Is it because they are weaker that we find it safe to take advantage of them and make life harder for them than for ourselves? How manly we are.

If these two women had homesteads of their own, the money they pay in rent would hire men to do the work for them.

—*W.H.McMaster, Indian Head*
Letter to the Editor
Grain Growers' Guide, *1909*

Washing day on Wyman's farm, near Bon Accord, Alberta, circa 1918

How many men ever thought that the present homestead law is unfair, even to men themselves? Here are two farmers, pioneer homesteaders, the family of one consisting of sons, the other of daughters—a common case in the west. In a few years the man with the sons spreads out, homesteads right and left, gobbling up a wide area of land; the man with the daughters cannot extend his homestead rights.

The accident of sex in the family enriches one and impoverishes the other. The law steps in and provides a birth-right dowry for the man having sons, and none for the man with daughters.

Miss Georgina Binnie-Clark, an Englishwoman of moderate means, considerable culture, unusual enterprise, and rare pluck, on behalf of herself and numbers of her single country-women similarly situated, came in the summer of '06 to experiment in farming in the Canadian West. Her first move was to interview the Dominion Government to secure a free homestead. She had references to show that she had means to prosecute farming successfully, should she be entrusted with a free farm. The Government was obdurate. She could get nothing. Undaunted she turned westward to investigate, and finally finding a discouraged farmer in the Qu'Appelle Valley, she bought outright his whole plant, including farm, machinery, crop, two cows and three horses, and started in to work, breaking twenty-five acres with a sulky plow in the first season. She lived entirely alone through the long bitter winter of '06-'07, getting her own wood, caring wholly for her own stock, two miles from any neighbour, and had a dog and revolver for her body-guard.

Miss Binnie-Clark still prosecutes farming in the west and continues to make a brilliant success of it. She does not do the heavy work herself. She hires a man and his wife, and she makes it pay just as so many bachelors do. Possessed of some means, it was not her intention to continue at the heavy work; she simply experimented to know exactly what it was and to prove that woman in an emergency could farm were she so minded.

Women should have the right to homestead if they desire to do so. Have they not helped to develop this western country and should they not have equal privileges with their sisters south of us? And would it not help to solve the problem of lessening the number of bachelors' halls that dot our prairies?

—*Isabelle Beaton Graham*
Grain Growers' Guide
November 17, 1909

*Cora Hind
examining crop*

There was a rich farmer once, who died possessed of three very fine farms of three hundred and twenty acres each. He left a farm to each of his three sons. To his daughter Martha, a woman of forty years of age, the eldest of the family—he left a cow and one hundred dollars. The wording of the will ran: "To my dear daughter, Martha, I leave the sum of one hundred dollars, and one cow named 'Bella'."

How would you like to be left at forty years of age, with no training and very little education, facing the world with one hundred dollars and one cow, even if she were named 'Bella'?

—*Nellie McClung*
In Times Like These

We have to get the vote on account of the laws. In Ontario a woman has some claim on her husband's property, but none here. That was changed because of Indian wives. The poor Indian women were cut off from any claim on a man's property. They said they had to do away with the wife's claim too, on account of the boom in 1882 when property was changing hands so fast. But it won't be set right until women vote. You'll see.

—*Nellie McClung*
Clearing In The West

MRS. DOWLER—MRS. STEVENSON:
"Whereas women are taxed for the support of the Government the same as the men, and in this present time of stress women are urged to get out on the land to produce food;
"Therefore, we feel that any natural resources that the Government has to put at the disposal of its citizens should be free to all, irrespective of sex, and
"We most respectfully ask that Homesteading privileges be extended to women on an equality with men."
—Carried.

—*Resolution presented to a convention of the United Farm Women of Alberta, 1918*

Milking, Elk Valley, Alberta

I for one would never have gotten discouraged so quickly if I could have seen anything coming to me for all I was going through on a homestead, although my husband repeatedly told me he would give me my share. I felt that wasn't what I wanted. I felt I wanted the law to grant us our share as well as the men. I felt humbled to take anything off my husband in a way although I knew it was rightly mine. I always felt I wanted the law to make it straight for me.

—Letter from Elizabeth Clark of Nanaimo, B.C.,
to Premier Scott of Saskatchewan
January 16, 1913

We are told that a son "earns or helps to earn the land", therefore, the land is sacredly reserved for him. The daughter can't earn anything at home, so there's nothing saved for her. She is compelled to stay there, however, and work from year's end to year's end, but—"there's no money in her work." It would be sheer folly to dower a daughter when the law doesn't compel him and he makes the law himself. It's all quite easy....we are required to accept the proposition, that "the boys earn the land and it should be given to them", and so "we grow more corn to feed more pigs to buy more land to grow more corn to feed more pigs to buy more land, etc., *ad infinitum*, all for our sons, whom in our short-sightedness we place upon pedestals with our own work-hardened hands, then stand back and admiringly exclaim, "behold how splendidly they have climbed to their eminence!"And we have heartlessly robbed our daughters and wives and mothers to place the sons there. We could pay a hired man per agreement and get rid of him; we cannot settle with the son, except by giving him all there is—land, furnishings, sister's and mother's share—everything in sight. How level-headed we are. How just we are.

—Isobel,
"Around the Fireside"
Grain Growers' Guide

Stooking, Milo area, circa *1923*

The Story of Jennie and John Tightwad,
In Installments

I

John Tightwad, bachelor, in the Pleasant Valley district, Saskatchewan, suddenly bethought him of the joys of a home and the comfort of woman-cooked meals, whereupon he packed his telescope and went East for the winter. He had definite designs upon the liberty of one Jenny Armstrong, and finding her the same jolly capable Jennie she used to be, he enlarged to her upon the great future of the West and finally put the proposition of taking up residence there boldly before her. Jennie consented and they were married. In the process John promised to endow her with all his worldly goods. The fact that they consisted of one homestead, a little cold, leaky-roofed shack, a yoke of oxen, and some machinery with chattel mortgages against it, did not dim the splendour of the promise in Jennie's eyes. She set out for her new home with a heart beating high with hope.

—Grain Growers' Guide
October 14, 1914

II

The first year of her married life Jennie Tightwad found that what she had looked upon in the past as hard labor had been luxurious leisure compared with her present employment. She worked early and late, helping John in the fields when her work was done in the house. John Tightwad was one of those terrific workers who, feeling no physical limitations himself, is intolerant of them in others.

That fall, thru their combined efforts, they cleared off a large part of the debt on the hired machinery. Jennie had saved her husband the salary of a hired man, which might fairly be reckoned at twenty-five dollars a month and the hired man's board at another ten dollars a month, making in all a saving of about two hundred and forty-five dollars for the seven months hired help has generally to be kept. She did less work than a hired man, certainly, but relieving her husband of household responsibility she enabled him to do more.

She was not offered any of the crop returns nor was she consulted about the disposition of them. John told her in a general way what he was going to do with the money.

—Grain Growers' Guide
November 2, 1914

II   Getting Down to Realities

ɪ The Courtship

III

The second year of their married life the home of John and Jennie Tightwad was brightened by the arrival of young Bob. Jennie's outdoor activities were curtailed by this event, but her heart was made to blossom like the rose and she and John renewed their courtship in their common joy over their little son.

But Jennie was no shirk, and in order to do her full share towards getting along milked a cow and kept enough hens, and made enough garden and sold enough butter to supply the table and buy the very few clothes she and the baby indulged in.

So this year Jennie added a son to the potential earning power of the family and saved a hundred dollar store bill and still she did not handle any of the money nor was she consulted as to its disposition. It was all John's money.

—Grain Growers' Guide
October 28, 1914

III Contributes the Keep of the House

IV

Fifteen years drifted along and at the end of that time John Tightwad owned 2 sections of land, clear, many head of stock, a splendid barn, a fair sized house and six children. All that Jennie owned of this was her rather dowdy wardrobe. She hadn't even a legal share in the children. When she wanted money she had to beg John to let her have it and there was always a scene and a wrangle. He made it very clear to her that the money, and the house and the family were all his, tho she had grown horny-handed in working for them.

Jennie at last declared that she wouldn't stand it and consulted a lawyer. She found that her husband was quite within the law. She had no legal claim on anything. She discovered, to her chagrin, that her position in the home of her husband all these years had been that of an unpaid domestic.

—Grain Growers' Guide
November 11, 1914

IV Just a Domestic

V

Three years passed and the financial relations between John and Jennie Tightwad became more and more strained. In addition a new anxiety over-shadowed the home. Rumours began to reach Jennie of John's attentions to a certain pretty widow who had taken up residence in the district.

One day John announced curtly that he was going away for two or three days on business. About the time she was expecting him back a neighbor drove up to the house and broke the news to her as gently as he could that John had disappeared with the widow after having sold his farm, stock, house and furniture to a wealthy American speculator. He was safely out of reach, and now the law which, during her residence with her husband refused her any claim on her children, suddenly changed its tactics and demanded that she support them, after they were turned off the homestead.

With the help of some compassionate neighbors she got a little house in town and a few pieces of furniture and began to take in washing for a living.

—Grain Growers' Guide
November 18, 1914

v Destitution

Dear Sir:

There are lots of cases where men leave their wives and run away with other women leaving their wives destitute. As he has married her and so prevented her from earning her own living, as there are generally little ones to support, it is only fair that she should have the right to some of his property after his death, and also some say as to whether her home is sold or not....

As to springing it on you all of a sudden, that is folly as we want everyone to know of the way the law now stands...a man can sell everything and leave his wife and children penniless...Is it fair that a woman work all her life and then perhaps be left without a cent of what she has helped to earn? Methinks I hear the echo of the shout from many throats No! No!! No!!!

—*"Lord Ullin's Daughter"*
Grain Growers' Guide
February, 1909

REPLY TO LORD ULLIN'S DAUGHTER

The farmer stands at the altar, he has experience of farming, of business, of the world; the young wife has little or none, but henceforth she is to decide for him what is right and best and can say "yes" or "no" to his will in flat contradiction to the vow lately made—"to obey".

I oppose the dower for, having a number of sons, one of them at least is pretty sure to marry a woman who would use the dower law very unjustly, to his disadvantage. Is it right that property I leave him shall be controlled by any crank of a woman he may marry?

The dower remedy is worse than the ill it is to cure, and creates other injustice, tyranny, and home dissensions.

—Grain Growers' Guide
August 7, 1909

"Why should women worry about possessing some of their husband's property during his lifetime?" he asked. "Time enough after he's dead!"

—*Hon. Charles W. Cross, Attorney-General of Alberta*
Emily Murphy, Crusader

Haymaking

Moosomin, Saskatchewan
May 14, 1915

Hon. Walter Scott, Regina, Sask.

Dear Sir:
I beg of you in the name of justice to women that you give them your most careful consideration and urge upon your Government the necessity of passing a law at this session to give a married woman a legal and equal right to the property they have jointly accumulated....why should a man have the legal right to will even 1/2 of their joint earnings to his friends, especially where there are no children....That is what I get in return for my work, money and most of all my entire devotion to a man for 24 1/2 years. And yet the law does not allow me anything better. He is figuring now on selling out in the fall....He says he has enough to keep him alright and I can rustle for myself....All I get is the product of the hens and I have to keep the house in groceries first and whatever is left over I can have for myself. Although last year he took $10.00 from me, and the year before he took $3.00 and that means a lot to me when I have so little to do with. He says the hens are his as he feeds them so I do not own a hen after all these years of toil and sacrifice according to our Western laws. One year ago I was completely done up. I worked on until I could not stand up without fainting....I never got...1/2 day rest, not even a holiday since 1909....

Now you may ask why did I do all this hard work? My reply is simple. I had no choice in the matter. I was forced to it. I either had to do it or walk out penniless and so I have just held on for the 6 years waiting patiently for the Government of Sask. to wake up and do justice to its women slaves. It may be the Government does not really know the true condition of affairs although I have been told repeatedly that very sad cases have been brought before the Sask. Govt. several times by the L.C. of Regina....

Jennie White

Carnduff
February 12, 1913

To Mr. Scott
Dear Sir:
i though i would you to let you know that i am in faver of the Dowere law and i am shure there are others who would be glad to have it Only they dont know were to write to it is a shame the way some are used i think it is high time that drink is put down and cep down, when a woman works for 25 years out side and in and her husband put all the profet in the hotell and thire is lots of that around hear, and now i will trust to your Honer to do all you cand and God will Bless you,

Yours trully
Mrs. Noble Hodgson

Domestic scene

Dundurn, Sask.

To the Honorable Walter Scott

We gather from a woman's page in the Winnipeg Weekly Free Press that efforts are being made to secure a dower law in the coming session of Parliament. The chief items of the proposed law that we object to, as the women demand it, are that men can no longer deal with their land as heretofore. Although in nearly all cases the farm and whole outfit are the man's before his marriage, the women are demanding that practically the power over it shall be taken from him, that the wife shall have the power to override the husband's wishes respecting a mortgage or sale of any of it, that the wife shall have half the farm on his death....

To these points we have great objections for we think them very unjust. I may say I am writing on behalf of the Farmers Anti-Dower Law Association. We call our organization "The Farmer's" because 90 percent of landowners are farmers, and it is this class of men that are aimed at....

I may say my association can see no desire or demand by farmers for this law that a large number are quite opposed to it, and would vote against any government passing such a law that the bulk of farmers wives do not desire the law....

> *I am Sir*
> *Truly Yours*
> *W. Hordern*
> *Secretary of the Farmers Association*

Sir, I see in your January number of the Grain Growers' Guide a Saskatchewan farmer draws the attention of your readers to the movement being made in regard to the dower for married women....We are asking for one-third of whatever our husbands are worth and the right of refusing or consenting to the selling or mortaging of the same, the dower law not helping us at all as long as our husbands are living.

Then he says nine out of ten farmers do not marry until they are worth so much and that we don't help to make the farm. Then what allowance does he make for the homesteader, that is the married man who comes we will say from England? He is only a poor man with nothing to start with. Do you think his wife sits beside the stove while her husband makes the farm? No; she just hires out and throws her earnings into the common purse. Then he says we are only aiming at the farmer. That too, is untrue, as our petitions apply to all men; and I have now on my petition doctors, tradesmen, etc., all who are willing signers. I am drawing on to two hundred signers...

> —*A Farmer's Wife*
> Grain Growers' Guide
> *May, 1909*

Women mowing and raking hay, 1916

The Hon. Walter Scott, Regina, Sask.

Dear Sir:
I beg to extend to you my deepest gratitude and sincerest appreciation of what you and your colleagues have done for the women of Saskatchewan....

I am pleased to tell you that these bills [prohibition and the Homestead Act] are bearing fruit already. In one home a few miles from here a man who had been drinking heavily during the last 4 or 5 years drove his wife from home at the point of a gun, though he had not had any liquor for a week or ten days. Then he was going to sell out but when he found he could not sell without her consent, he calmed down and sent for her to come back and said he would try and do better. So we hope the Dower Law has saved one home already from being wrecked.

Jennie White

July 1, 1918

Dear Miss Stocking:
Well, things are the same, I have just as hard a time to get a dollar out of my husband as ever. I don't get a thing unless I sew for it, and it is rather hard on me to have to do that and the work besides.

I went to Regina one day last week and I stayed in to see a lawyer. He told me that law is to that effect that a man don't have to give his wife any money if he don't want to. I also asked him about woman's right in the homestead all right while she is living on same, but the husband has a right to rent a house some place else and move his wife into it, and then sell the homestead after she is moved. I was much surprised to know this. Now, what good are these homestead rights in the home for wives if this can take place—simply no good whatever. A mean husband will do anything. I know a man not far from here that moved his wife into town last year, and then he turned round and sold his homestead, and went to the States with the money....She had to take in washing to support five children. So this is what such law mean.

It is just terrible that a poor wife can be used like this, in this country where we got to work so hard. This matter should be taken up, and worked upon very quickly. Can you look into this, Miss Stocking? Also that a right of the farm money. My husband takes off pretty good crops every year, but he will never give me anything in the fall, or any other time. We have three sons grown up now, and he will supply them with all the money they can spend, but I must not have any, and I have worked so hard to help to earn the farm. It is not fair.

Well, I must close now, hoping to hear from you soon, I am

Your sincere friend,
Mrs. F. Stewart

P.S. I forgot to tell you that this lawyer said that a wife had no right whatever to any of her husband's property nor money in this country, under the present law.

Seeding turnips on the Harrison farm near Cochrane, Alberta

Because the work of the married woman, in caring for her household, was supposed to be a labor of love, and of no economic value....women were at first content to sell their work at far below its real value, and thus depress the wage scale for all workers. Today women have proved themselves capable of entering many fields of labor, manual and intellectual, in which men work, and their demand for equal opportunity, and equal pay for equal work is being more and more recognised. Until it is fully recognised, women's work will always have a tendency to hold down the standard of wages, and displace men...Perhaps no group of women have suffered more from this condition of affairs than the Farm women. Certainly no group of women has labored so hard so ungrudgingly and so unselfishly. And yet we know for a fact that in many instances, not even the produce that they raise by their own labor, can be sold and claimed as their own. Can such a humiliating condition be conducive to a happy married life, or a right environment in which to bring up children? And it is not so uncommon a condition as might be supposed. Our law is little or no protection to the married woman; the Dower Act is of little value. The Community Property Act introduced at the last session was the embryo from which some satisfactory legislation may result. Modern conditions must be faced, and the wife must not be placed in an inferior economic position to the unmarried woman, because she gives herself to the valuable and important work of caring for home and family.

> —*Irene Parlby*
> Alberta Labor Annual
> *September 5, 1925*

BILL
No. 54 of 1925
*An Act Establishing Community Property as between
Husband and Wife....*

3. All property of the husband (or wife) owned by him (or her) before marriage and that acquired afterward by gift...shall be his (or her) separate property...

5. All other property acquired by either husband or wife, or both, during the marriage, including the rents and profits of the separate property of the husband and wife, shall be community property....

8. The husband shall have the management and control of the community property with the like absolute power of disposition, other than testamentary, over community personal property as he has of his separate estate; but he shall not sell, convey or encumber the community real estate unless the wife joins with him in executing the instrument of conveyance....

—from a bill introduced into the Alberta Legislature in 1925, but never passed into law.

Irene
Parlby

VI Winning The Vote

Ontario had the first women's suffrage movement in Canada, but the prairie provinces had the first women voters. In 1916, the three western governments tripped over one another in a gallant rush to extend the franchise (and grab a share of public acclaim). Each chivalrous premier claimed "first place" for his party and province: in Manitoba for extending the franchise, in Alberta for enacting political equality at all levels of government; and in Saskatchewan for giving women the first chance to use their new powers. But despite this simultaneous success, the women's suffrage movements in the three provinces operated independently of one another, each developing its own techniques and style.

Because western settlement began in Manitoba, the women's movement did too. A group of Icelandic women organized a suffrage league in the 1890's, and the Women's Christian Temperance Union took up the cause some time before 1893. Under the determined leadership of pioneer physician Dr. Amelia Yeomans, the WCTU passed pro-suffrage resolutions, gathered petitions and staged a public debate, only to be humiliated in 1894, when the MLA who sponsored a women's suffrage resolution didn't bother to have it printed for debate in the Provincial Assembly. There they were, dozens of women in the balcony, waiting, one imagines, with restless anticipation, and all their "champion" had to say was "not printed". That experience provoked Dr. Yeomans, by then provincial president for the Ontario-based Dominion Women's Enfranchisement Association, to organize the Manitoba Equal Franchise Club, which worked quietly for several years until Dr. Yeomans moved away from Winnipeg and interest waned.

When the movement revived a decade later, only one of the orginal leaders, E. Cora Hind, remained active. A new generation of women was starting from scratch. In 1906, Catherine Simpson-Hays of the *Winnipeg Free Press* had convened a national meeting of newspaperwomen to formally establish the Canadian Women's Press Club, one of the first associations for professional women. The Winnipeg branch was a vigorous group, which included Lillian Beynon Thomas and her sister Francis M.Beynon, E. Cora Hind, Mae Clendennan, Nellie McClung and Kennethe Haig. In 1912, a few of these women tried to shock the Manitoba government into improving the working and living conditions of women factory workers. Instead, the Premier's indifference shocked the press women into seeking the vote. And so the Winnipeg (later Manitoba) Political Equality League was formed in 1912, with support from the WCTU and the Manitoba Grain Growers.

The climax of the League's publicity campaign was a head-on confrontation with the conservative government of Sir Rodmond Roblin. Unable to enlist an MLA to work on their behalf in the House, a League delegation presented their case in person, and were rudely lectured by the Premier for their trouble. They couldn't have asked for better treatment, for the next day, January 28, 1914, the women staged a riotous "mock parliament" at the Walker Theatre in Winnipeg. When the *men* came to beg for the vote, "Premier" Nellie McClung dismissed them with a parody of Roblin's outburst in the Legislature the day before. The performance was an outstanding polemical and financial success.

In just two years, the League had made women's suffrage a major political issue, one which the Manitoba Liberals could and did use against the Roblin Conservatives. With the active campaign support of suffrage leaders, the Liberals came to power in August 1915. On January 28, 1916, during the new government's first session, Manitoba women were enfranchised—but not until they had proven their desire for the reform with a 40,000-name petition. Francis Beynon reflected on the struggle:

> An easy victory some people say, who looking on from a safe distance, have no conception of the drudgery that...was undergone by the members of the Political Equality League in its four strenuous years of life. Nor do they take into account the fact that this was merely final outcropping of a sentiment which has been patiently fostered by one society after another for more than twenty years.

If anything, Saskatchewan women achieved their success with even more drudgery and more patience. For one thing, there was no central core of urban women to coordinate the campaign as there had been in Manitoba. For another, the government always gave the movement a kind of mealy-mouthed support. This put the suffragists in Saskatchewan at a psychological disadvantage compared to their sisters in Manitoba. Instead of crusading for good against evil, they had to cater to the whims of Premier Walter Scott, who assured them that the tasks he set them were all for their own good.

Except for the WCTU, the first women's suffrage advocates in Saskatchewan were men. In 1912, the Saskatchewan Grain Growers' Association petitioned the government to enfranchise women. Later that year, MLA J.E. Bradshaw introduced a suffrage resolution in the Legislature. The discussion was alternately facetious and fatuous, but in the end the government declared its readiness to enfranchise women, as soon as the women themselves demonstrated their interest.

In the next year, about 2,500 women took up the challenge. Working on their own initiative, in isolation from one another, farm women obtained petition forms from the SGGA or wrote letters to the Premier. Despite this display of interest, Scott's standard response was the same as ever: women do not want to vote. Finally, Francis Beynon wrote to ask how many signatures it would take to convince him: "There must have been some misunderstanding,"he stated in effect. "I could not extend the franchise on the say-so of the women; I'd need the approval of the electorate." For "electorate" read "the men".

Meanwhile, the temperance forces were looking to women for support. Insulted by a suggestion that women ought to be allowed to vote only on provincial liquor referenda, and not in general elections, the temperance unions prepared a petition calling for full women's suffrage. Their work was accelerated in 1915 by the formation of the Provincial Equal Franchise Board, a province-wide alliance of suffrage workers. On May 27, within four months of its inauguration, the Board presented the Legislature with its 10,000 signatures, gathered from organized farm women, city clubwomen, and the temperance unions. Premier Scott was moved to oratory, but not to action. The House was busy with "exceedingly important issues", he said.

Nothing more was heard from Scott until the following December, when he suggested that the women gather some more names. Then a month later, he abruptly announced that equal suffrage would be enacted immediately. As he frankly admitted, Saskatchewan didn't want to lag behind Manitoba and Alberta. So on Valentine's Day, 1914, when the PEFB returned with another 10,000 names, Premier Scott was ready with a positive answer, and another dose of patronizing twaddle: had he known he was sending the poor ladies out into unusually severe January cold, he would never have "consented" to their petition gathering. Saskatchewan women were enfranchised on March 14, 1916.

Alberta followed suit on April 19, after six years of sporadic petitioning by the WCCTU, UFWA, Equal Franchise League, Local Councils of Women, Women's Canadian Clubs and Women's Institutes. None of the groups made much of a splash until 1914 when the Edmonton Equal Franchise League and the Calgary Local Council of Women presented a 12,000 name petition to Premier Sifton, who was polite but unenthusiastic. The petitioners hadn't canvassed any farm women, Sifton pointed out. The next year, the city women returned with country allies, but Sifton remained noncommittal. Then, in the fall of 1915, for no reason that could be determined from the outside, he promised the extension of full political rights for women at the next legislative session. The bill became law on April 19, 1916.

Leaders of the agitation in Alberta included UFWA

president Irene Parlby, later Minister without Portfolio in the United Farmers' Government; clubwomen Emily Murphy and Alice Jamieson, both of whom were subsequently appointed magistrates; and temperance workers Louise McKinney and Nellie McClung (who moved to Alberta in 1914), who were later elected to the Alberta Legislature.

Obviously, suffragists in the three provinces had much in common despite the accidents of political history which determined the course of their campaigns. The leadership of the WCTU and the backing of farm and labour movements were universal. So was the wide diffusion of pro-suffrage sentiment: votes for women became a popular cause on the prairies as nowhere else in Canada. Why? Because of women's contribution as pioneers? Because of the populist philosophy of the farm movement? Because loneliness and social conditions had encouraged prairie women to band together? Because wartime propaganda raised the status of women at just the right time? Because of leaders like Francis Beynon and Nellie McClung? Whatever the reasons, the prairie suffrage movement prospered not only among a coterie of radicals, as it typically did elsewhere in Canada, but in the minds and homes of "ordinary" western women as well.

Given this healthy beginning, one might have anticipated a strong, united assault on the next barricade—the Dominion Elections Act which excluded women from federal politics. An attempt was made to organize a national campaign, but in the end, individual associations worked independently and spasmodically. In January, 1919, the federal franchise was extended to all Canadian women, regardless of their provincial status.

TO BE ATTRACTIVE IS WOMAN'S MAIN DUTY

Dear Miss Beynon:

I find that I am strictly orthodox, and believe that man was intended by nature to take the initiative in all things, and that woman was made to help him, mostly as an inspiration. I believe that it is woman's business to be as attractive as nature or art will let her, that she should never over-tax her powers at work, and that the preservation of her attractions is one of her main duties. Men naturally admire beauty and feminine graces, women admire strength. This is instinctive, and, so far as the sexes are related to each other, instinct governs. Women, the trouble is that we are raising a brood of weaklings. Debilitated by vices, encouraged in laziness and ignorance, allowed an un-Christian and unwarranted license in morals, the average man is the disgrace of his mother; so much so, that women must take the helm. Lower than animals! I do not selfishly wish the vote for myself. I want to see a race of men raised who are unquestionably able to fight menacing dragons, whether it be white slavery, drink, or oppression. Men, are you men or mice? Are you willing to do this...or shall we spit in your faces, as the squaws did when the braves returned scalpless from the battle?

Yours for the welfare of the race,

W.W.

—Grain Growers' Guide
October 1, 1913

W.W.'s theory that a woman should appeal to a man through her basest qualities—her vanity, her weakness, for which a more honest word is incompetence; her mental dependence, which is either ignorance or stupidity, revolts me, more especially as these attributes appeal to the basest side of man's nature—his vanity, his sensual passions and his arrogance. I refuse to believe that such a low appeal is necessary.

How can the woman who has to wheedle or coax or scheme or look pretty to get from her husband what she has honestly earned, give her child any real moral stamina or high sense of honor? We want a new spirit of national motherhood—mothers whose love for their own children teaches them love for all children; mothers who will not boast of their weakness but seek for strength to fight the battle for their own and their neighbours' children; mothers who are more concerned with raising the moral and intellectual standards of the community in which they live than in applying the latest suggestions of the beauty doctor. The ballot is one weapon in this fight for the health, chastity and life of these children....I regard it as an obligation on the part of every woman to arm herself with this weapon....

—*Francis Beynon*
Grain Growers' Guide
October 1, 1913

From Grain Growers' Guide, *July 8, 1914*

The object of keeping the franchise from women is political. The men who mold public opinion are afraid the laws which women would make would not be to the liking or interest of the men who now dominate legislation. Most men who deny the right of voting to their wives and daughters would have as cheerfully denied it to their hired men, and for a similar reason.

—Grain Growers' Guide
September 22, 1909

I am not among those who were anxious for the franchise—on the contrary I shrank from it. It is only within the last few years I have favoured it at all. It was witnessing the conditions of less fortunate women than myself that awakened me to the selfishness of holding back from others a power which might help them remedy their unhappiness....

—Mrs. Motherwell
Speech to Homemaker's Club
Lunburg, Saskatchewan
December 5, 1916

Men alone are not capable of making laws for men and women. Laws are made from man's standpoint. There is a law in this province whereby a man can sell all he has without the knowledge or consent of his wife, and can skip out, leaving her and her children without anything. There is a law by which a man can will away all his property and leave his wife nothing. There is a law by which a father is heir to his child's property. Children have only one legal guardian, only one parent in the eyes of the law, and that parent is the father. Such laws as these are on the statute books, yet people will say that women should trust to man's chivalry.

—Nellie McClung
Newspaper report
May 20, 1915

Without doubt the democracy of the twentieth century demands the wisdom, sympathy and insight of woman for its full development, and Canadian women cannot set themselves too soon to the solution of the problems now affecting the economic and social well-being of the Dominion. Most men are free to confess that they have made more or less of a botch of trying to run the government by themselves. We look for a new moral impetus, a saner outlook and wider human sympathy to enter into the settlement of our public questions with the advent of women into public affairs.

—Grain Growers' Guide
February 4, 1914

Manitoba Equal Suffrage Club executive, 1900; (left to right) Cora Hind, Mrs. A.E. Henry, Mrs. Maude E. Mills, Mrs. Mary Hislop, Maggie Young, Amelia Yeomans (president)

I believe the woman in politics would be quite like the man in politics. I suppose good women might go to the polls without actual loss of dignity, but if they mixed in "practical politics" they would have to learn a lot about discarding their best ideals. And they would learn it—women are quick at intrigue, and an unscrupulous woman is ever more merciless than any man....I am convinced that the whole secret of woman's clamoring for her rights lies in the pocketbook.... Men want to give women "what money they need"—they propose to be the judges of this, and women, year by year, have grown more weary of it, more desirous of having things more equitably arranged. Now on this one point I am a suffragist. If by voting we could settle this unlovely dispute, remove from women's lives this cloud of unhappiness, I would say, let us vote. Let us go to the polls with the babies in our arms and the little ones tagging after. But I cannot see how suffrage would make this matter any better. If the law should name a certain percentage of a man's salary as the just portion for a woman's services as his partner in life, there would still be room for dispute....So long as Marriage remains an Institution, so long as men and women mate together with the idea of keeping to each other for a life time, these questions of domestic equity will come up and they will have to be settled by the couple themselves. No law can intervene here. I think most women would vote with their husbands—I know all unmarried women would vote with their sweethearts—I never saw a girl who wouldn't change her politics to suit her lover. The women who write to me about my shortcomings on the suffrage question invariably say to me: "You are too bright a woman—you have too good a mind to remain dense on the suffrage question." I insist that I am not dense about it. I declare that suffrage would cut very little figure in my life, and I am not ashamed nor afraid to say so. I am a woman. I like my home. I like to see the rooms straightened up and to have three meals a day and a general air of domestic life around me. It may be a galling thing to women to admit it, but Nature provided man with wider liberty than woman. No legislation nor change of custom can ever alter this fact. There is not, and never can be, any natural equality between man and woman. Whenever you find a woman who can go among men as one of them, making herself a mere automaton, a thinking box, a business machine, you find a creature who is not a woman at all. Men can be natural in business with each other. Between men and men and between women and women there is a natural sex understanding that need not be curbed nor guarded. But between men and women sex is the danger point. I have nothing against the business woman. I admire her courage and her self-control; nevertheless, I say her position is unnatural if it takes her, all day long, into a world of men. If we have a generation of girls who would rather support themselves than marry, and wives who would rather be breadwinners than mothers, Nature must have made a dreadful mistake...

—Grain Growers' Guide
August 21, 1909

"The Door Steadily Opens", from the Grain Growers' Guide, *September 21, 1910*

"Now you forget all this nonsense about women voting," Premier Roblin [of Manitoba] went on in his suavest tones. "You're a fine, smart young woman, I can see that. And take it from me, nice women don't want the vote."

His voice dripped fatness.

"By nice women," I said, "you probably mean selfish women who have no more thought for the underpaid, overworked women than a pussycat in a sunny window has for the starving kitten on the street. Now in that sense I am not a nice woman, for I do care. I care about those factory women, working in ill-smelling holes, and we intend to do something about it, and when I say 'we' I'm talking for a great many women, of whom you will hear more as the days go on."

—*Nellie McClung*
The Stream Runs Fast

On one occasion somebody called out to Nellie McClung "Where are your children, while you're out speaking?" She said, "My children are at home with their father—the only 'parent' the law allows." At that time mothers had no right to the children at all. A father could will away his child to somebody else!

—*Mrs. Rogers*
Past president, Alberta Women's Institute
Interview, 1924

The greatest argument against women's suffrage is that they can do so much by indirect influence. If they can do so much good by indirect influence, why can they not do much more good by direct influence.

—*Nellie McClung*
Newspaper report
May 20, 1915

Nellie McClung with son Mark

UNSEXED

It doesn't unsex her to toil in a factory,
Minding the looms from the dawn till the night,
To deal with a school-full of children refractory,
Doesn't unsex her in anyone's sight;
Work in a store, where her back aches inhumanly,
Doesn't unsex her at all, you will note,
But think how exceedingly rough and unwomanly
Woman would be, if she happened to vote!

To sweat in a laundry that's torrid and horrid(er)
Doesn't subtract from her womanly charm;
And scrubbing the floors in an echoing corridor
Doesn't unsex her, so where is the harm?
It doesn't unsex her to nurse us with bravery,
Loosing death's hand from its grip on the throat;
But ah', how the voices grow quivery, quavery,
Wailing: "Alas, 'twill unsex her to vote!"

She's feminine yet when she juggles the crockery,
Bringing you blithely the order you give;
Toil(ing) in sweat shops where life is a mockery,
Just for the pittance on which she can live;
That doesn't seem to unsex her a particle.
"Labor is noble"—so somebody wrote—
But ballots are known as a dangerous article,
"Woman's unsexed if you give her the vote!"

—Berton Braley
Grain Growers' Guide

NEGLECTING THE HOME

O, it isn't home-neglecting
You spend your time selecting
Seven blouses and a jacket and a hat
Or to give your day to paying
Needless visits, or to playing
Auction bridge. What critic could
Object to that?
But to spend two precious hours
At a lecture! Oh, my powers!
The home is all a woman needs to learn!
And an hour or a quarter,
Spent in voting! Why, my daughter,
The home would not be there on your return.

184

Group portrait taken at Nellie McClung's home in Edmonton; (centre) Nellie McClung, Mrs. Pankhurst, Mrs. Emily Murphy

The liquor traffic is unanimous declaring that woman's place is the home—and that politics are degrading to women; also that if women ever get the vote that homes will be neglected and poor little deficient children will be bereft of their mother's care.

Such sweet solicitude for home and children on the part of the liquor people is very kind and timely. Of course they do not mind keeping the fathers away from home, and degrading him so that he is not particularly pleasant company for the wife and children, but they are particular on one point—"She must stick around" as long as the home lasts anyway.

The opposition of the liquor traffic to Woman's Suffrage should convince all thinking people that granting the vote to women will have an effect on the temperance question—it is the one piece of legislation that the liquor people are afraid of and so they work against it insidiously and secretly, under the name of the Anti-Suffrage Association.

Of course there are many people opposing Suffrage from honest and pure motives; and these people are a perfect delight to the liquor people; and to all other agencies who live on the frailties of humanity.

—*Nellie McClung*
Newspaper report
January 13, 1914

In Carman, a small town between Manitou and Winnipeg, a vote on local option was coming and the liquor interests were afraid they would be defeated, for at that time women who had property in their own name could vote in municipal matters. And in Carman there were enough of these to swing the vote. The Conservative Government of Manitoba was appealed to by the Interests —couldn't they think of something? It would never do to let one town carry local option. The Government had resourceful advisers and they had a plan. They would quietly and without any flourish of trumpets, disfranchise the women.

When the voting day came and the women went out to vote they found their names were not on the list—no woman could vote—by Order in Council. I would like to have been there that day. There followed a reaction which frightened the powers, and from end to end of Manitoba a new movement began which ran like a prairie fire before a high wind. If the present Government would not give us a vote there was just one thing left for us to do. We would change the Government, and that is what we did, though it took a little time.

It was a bonny fight—a knock-down and drag-out fight, but it united the women of Manitoba in a great cause. I never felt such unity of purpose and I look on these days with great satisfaction. We really believed we were about to achieve a new world.

—*Nellie McClung*
The Stream Runs Fast

From Grain Growers' Guide, *November 29, 1916*

NELLIE McCLUNG

"She is not old, she is not young"
But a brave Irish lass is Nellie McClung
With a tongue that would soothe the birds off the trees
And bright sparkling eyes that shows she's a tease.
The ladies all love her, the men on her dote
But what's riling Miss Nellie is, they won't let her vote.

She asked Mr. Roblin and it sure grieved him bad
To refuse her a trifle, but it made Nellie mad
But Roblin knows Nellie, and, if he once let her vote
When the election was over, he would find he was smote.
And those bad wicked Grits, who are after his hide
Would smile in their sleeves when the old hero died.

Besides we all know, and the truth must be told,
Women's sphere is the home, not out in the cold
She's too tender and fragile to mix with the gang
Of Roblin's home guard who sometimes use slang
So while we are sorry it cannot be done—
Votes are for "Men only" not for Nellie McClung.

Nellie McClung

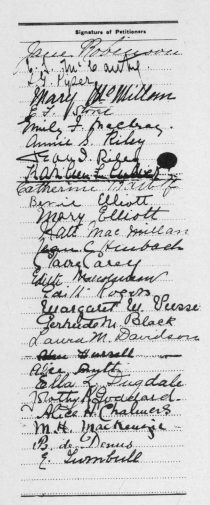

Signature of Petitioners

WOMEN SCORE IN DRAMA AND DEBATE

CLEVER SATIRE ON PROVINCIAL EVENTS IN MOCK PARLIAMENT

Petitions were first in order, and some facetious papers were read. One by the Society for the Prevention of Ugliness prayed that men wearing scarlet neckties, six inch collars and squeaky shoes be not allowed to enter any public building whatsoever. Mrs. W.C. Perry, Leader of the Opposition, then read a bill to confer dower rights on married men. In a clear, sympathetic voice, she made a strong appeal for poor, downtrodden men...

The Premier, Mrs. McClung, compared the gentlemanly conduct of the members of the delegation with the rabid courses of suffragists overseas. If all men were as intelligent as the leader of the delegation, she would have no hesitation in according them the suffrage. But such was unfortunately not the case. Mr. Skinner, with the customary hotheadedness of the reformer, had not stopped to think of that. Down to the south where men had the vote, it had been shown that seven-eights of Police Court offenders were men and only one-third of church members were men. "Another trouble is that if men start to vote, they will vote too much. Politics unsettles men, and unsettled men mean unsettled bills—broken furniture, broken vows and —divorce....It has been charged that politics is corrupt. I do not know how this report got out but I do most emphatically deny it. I have been in politics for a long time and I never knew of any division of public money among Members of the House, and you may be sure, if anything of that kind had been going on, I should have been in on it. Ladies and gentlemen, what I mean is that I would have known about it." At the end of her splendid address, Mrs. McClung was presented with a bouquet of red roses.

—Winnipeg Free Press
January 29, 1914

Presentation of Political Equality League petition for enfranchisement of women Manitoba, December 23, 1915; (top row) Mrs. A.V. Thomas, Mrs. F.J. Dixon; (bottom row) Dr. Mary Crawford, Mrs. Amelia Buvit

Mr. Scott, does your wife (if there is a Mrs. Scott) have to ask your permission to eat breakfast...or does your child have to cry for bread, no you give it, it is not a case of begging at all it is their lawful rights. ...Would you like to see us arise in a regiment and assail you with a club? Perhaps you are waiting to fill Regina Jail with window smashers. Nothing so degrading will happen for this reason we have an honorable government to deal with.

—Mary Mitchell
Rhein, Saskatchewan
Letter to Premier Scott of Saskatchewan
January 15, 1913

It may be difficult for you to believe it but the fact is that the evidence before me convinces me that it is only a small percentage of the women of Saskatchewan who have as yet given the question of women's suffrage any consideration at all and if the matter were put to the test I think it would be found that only a small fraction of our Sask. women would take the trouble to come out and vote upon it, yes or no.

—Reply from Premier Scott of Saskatchewan
July 19, 1914

SASKATCHEWAN WOMEN RECEIVE THE VOTE FROM SCOTT GOVERNMENT AT MEMORABLE ST. VALENTINE'S DAY ASSEMBLY

"THIS IS SO SUDDEN, SIR"

There was nothing remarkable in the scene that followed the acceptance by the premier of the appeal of the women. Loud applause, a waving of handkerchiefs, a short speech by the leader of the ladies coming straight from the heart, the singing of "They Are Jolly Good Fellows", and another epoch-making event had passed into history.

—Regina Leader
February 15, 1916

EQUAL RIGHTS FOR ALL

SONG

Words and Melody by

H. W. GOTHARD

Arranged by

J. W. BULLOUGH

—— 60 ——

Published by
United Farmers of Alberta
206 Lougheed Bldg.
Calgary, Alberta.

Suffrage song

ALBERTA

[In 1913] The Edmonton Political Equality League organized a meeting with [Premier] Sifton. They came down to the Legislature and there must have been 150 or 200 women. They gave a spiel, both Nellie [McClung] and Janey [Emily Murphy] spoke because they were both good speakers, but Sifton wouldn't let them go up the front steps to the Legislature. He stood on the second step and kept them standing around the well in the approach and he said to them, "did you ladies wash up your luncheon dishes before you came down here to ask me for votes?" He said, "if you haven't you'd better go home because you're not going to get any votes from me." He was most ungentlemanly. So the next session of the legislature was in Feb. (1914), a regular session, and I suggested to Mrs. Ferris that a better way would be to infiltrate the government so to speak and get possession of the building. So when 2 or 3 women appeared I took them in to see the interior of the building, and then 2 or 3 others came along casually and the first thing we knew we had the legislative hall filled with women. And they were sitting in the members' seats. Sifton couldn't call the police but he certainly gave them a piece of his mind. Anyway, they had won a point on him.

—*Tom Wilson*
1913 M.L.A. for Rocky Mountain House
Interview, 1967

ONE VOICE WAS RAISED AGAINST THE BILL
Boudreau Courageous

During the debate which followed the speech in which [Alberta] Premier Sifton introduced the second reading of the government measure [enacting political rights for women] Lucien Boudreau stepped into a niche of fame alongside his leader. He was the only member of the fifty-six to vote against granting women equality. Mr. Boudreau, fearless champion of a lost cause, sturdily voiced the sentiments which perhaps many of the present legislators felt but lacked the courage to make public....After the session a number of members took the honorable member for St. Albert away in a corner and jointly and severally congratulated him on his courage, whispering that he had expressed their sentiments exactly and they wished they might dare display his courage.

—Calgary Morning Albertan
March 2, 1916

At the last session of the Saskatchewan Legislature Premier Scott expressed himself as in favor of extending the franchise to women, but did not care to enact the necessary legislation until the women of Saskatchewan asked for it. It is now up to the women to "SPEAK" in clear and unmistakable terms.

From Grain Growers' Guide, *February 26, 1913*

Things are coming our way! Without any noise or fuss or trouble Woman Suffrage is arriving!...We rejoice particularly for the sake of the many unknown and unnamed workers who against the greatest discouragements, tried to do their little bit, and were many times ridiculed, criticized and misjudged by the very people they were trying to help, that is, other women.

—Nellie McClung
Manuscript, personal papers

We were the equal of men then in the vote and we sort of neglected using that equal right....Instead of just lining up when an election came, and marking your ballot with an X like your husband did (it just doubled the results of an election) we should have at least made more study of the legislation in our provinces and in the dominion, and became active prior to marriage in discussing things...that the women's lib parties seem to be fighting for now. We should have started it right then when we passed the franchise act, in my opinion.

—Cornelia Wood
M.L.A. for 25 years
Interview, 1974
Stony Plain, Alberta

The day that woman's suffrage became 'un fait accompli' in Alberta, Mrs. [Alice] Jamieson was in Edmonton. When the news came through that the women of the province had been granted the franchise, she rushed to the phone and called up two of her friends, both very prominent women in Canada and tireless workers for suffrage, Judge Emily Murphy and Mrs. Nellie McClung. The trio held a caucus and decided that they must celebrate in some way. "Being women," says Mrs. Jamieson, "we couldn't very well express our joy and satisfaction by going out and getting a bottle, so as we walked down Jasper avenue with our arms interlocked, Mrs. Murphy suggested that the most rash thing we could do would be to have our pictures taken."

—Dorothy Bowman Barker
Newspaper report

Nellie McClung, Alice Jamieson, Emily Murphy

There are two courses open to women. The first one is to line up with the two principal parties, just slide into the one that is most convenient, taking which one comes handiest. If they do this, the most appreciable difference their entry into politics will be that the voters' list is doubled in size, the cost of elections likewise increased.

Evidently they should be able to add something other than mere bulk. There is another way. Not as easy to follow for it requires courage and thinking, but everything in life that is worth while requires that. Instead of dividing into twos and fours and marching together until election day, and then dividing into two opposing forces, why can't we new voters, who have no political past to bind us, stand together, a great independent body of intelligent, thinking, investigating, open-minded, unprejudiced women, who weigh matters carefully, gathering up evidence, listening to all sides, with patience, with understanding, with charity; slow to think evil, ready to accord to each man his measure of praise and then acting fearlessly, courageously, without flavor of favor. Then would we truly become a terror to evildoers, a praise to them that do well.

> —*Nellie McClung*
> The Calgary News-Telegram
> *1917*

TILL THE GOAL IS WON

They are coming from the homestead,
 They are coming from the glen;
There are many thousands anxious
 For the call to vote again.
They are coming with a purpose,
 They are burning with desire,
That all men should share as equals,
 From the maiden to the sire.

We are calling to our women,
 That they join the forces strong;
And with shoulder close to shoulder
 We will surely right the wrong.
There is need of cleaner prospect
 In the ranks of public life;
We need those with purer motives,
 With a will to put down strife.

> —*by Mrs. A.P.Rainforth*
> *Spring Valley U.F.W.A.*

Group of women voting at Westcott, Alberta, 1917

EQUAL FRANCHISE LEAGUE
PLATFORM

1917, Province of Saskatchewan

1. SECURING OF FEDERAL FRANCHISE

2. ABOLITION OF PARTY POLITICS

Proven to be a factor in the production of graft and various other evils, which are, to a great extent, responsible for the deplorable economic conditions which exist in all lands where party politics predominate. This cannot be accomplished in a year but by having this as our objective, agitation will ultimately bring about the result.

3. SOCIAL AND MORAL REFORM

(a) Co-guardianship of parents. At present the mother is only the natural parent and has no legal standing as such, except in cases of illegitimate children when she is solely responsible.

(b) Equal property rights for husband and wife.

(c) Investigation and revision of laws regarding the responsibility of parents of illegitimate children.

(d) Equal wage for equal work.

(e) Minimum wage for girls and women.

(f) Maximum hours of labor per week for girls and women.

(g) Mothers' pensions. In cases where father dies and leaves a family dependent upon the mother, she should receive sufficient income from the Government to enable her to remain at home, instead of going out to labor and children placed in institutions or allowed to run the streets.

(h) Maternity allowance. A fixed sum should be available for every prospective mother. (In Australia $25.00 is allowed to every mother who presents a certificate of birth.)

(i) The absconding of either parent to be a criminal offence.

(j) Municipal nurses.

(l) State registration of nurses.

(m) Protection of persons of young womanhood to age of 21 years, making life at least as valuable as property.

An eminent speaker from the East, who visited one of our Western cities, a few years ago was filled with alarm when he found it was the Woman's Canadian Club he was billed to address, instead of the Men's. He said he could not address the women. He had no address that they could understand. The President tried to re-assure him by telling him it was surprising how much the women would be able to get if he would speak slowly!

—*Nellie McClung*
Manuscript, personal papers

Executive of the Saskatchewan Women Grain Growers: (back row) Mrs. Hawkes, Mrs. McNeal, Mrs. Flatt, Mrs. Ames, Mrs. Anderson, Mrs. Grant, Mrs. Haight, Mrs. Hicks; (seated) Mrs. Thompson, Mrs. McNaughton (president), Miss Stocking

Regina, Saskatchewan
November 29, 1919

Dear Mother and Father:

Well the ordeal of taking my seat in Parliament is all over, and my name goes down in Saskatchewan history. I was given a very warm welcome, and as one man said to me today I had attained an honor no other lady in Sask. could attain in being the first lady member. I have received many compliments and congratulations, but you can rest assured that it has not affected my head in the least and I only wish I was more worthy of the many nice things said about me. Everyone tells me I was so very calm and undisturbed as I went through the introduction, but if I looked that part I was not feeling that way. After I took my seat as a real member there was great applause and when the House adjourned I was surrounded by crowds of people waiting to meet me. A number of women's organizations was there from the city to extend a hearty welcome also Govt. members and private members. One woman's organization here in the city have invited me as Guest of Honor at a luncheon in one of the best hotels in the city next Thursday.

I was out at the Buildings this morning and to my great surprise here I was escorted to a special room with a card on the door, "Lady Members Room". That is something no other private member has. One Govt. official said to me it was all ready for me except the rocking chair and that was coming. This room of mine has nice table, large mirror, telephone, writing paper, easy chairs and I certainly appreciate very much the courtesy I am receiving. Max [Mr. Ramsland] had many friends here in Regina, and among the members of the Govt. and that is one reason for them being so kind to me, and although my position takes me among men and has since I began my campaign and entered into politics, but I was told by a man in Kamsack who opposed me and admitted he did that he heard it on every hand that although going into politics going through a hard campaign I had been a perfect lady in every way and I held the respect of every one by the lady-like way I conducted myself. I told him if for one moment I thought I could not be the same lady I had always tried to be I would never have entered politics. And I am sure my own good judgment will be used in every instance and my vote during my political (career) can never be bought.

...I miss the children but I know they are getting the best of care. This is nearly a book so I must close...

Lovingly,
Sod [Sarah Ramsland]

SOLDIERS AND NURSES FROM ALBERTA!!

You will have TWO VOTES at the forthcoming Election under the Alberta Military Representation Act.

GIVE ONE VOTE TO THE MAN OF YOUR CHOICE AND
THE OTHER TO THE SISTER.

LOOK

FOR

No. 14

ON YOUR

BALLOT PAPER!

LOOK

FOR

No. 14

ON YOUR

BALLOT PAPER!

MISS ROBERTA CATHERINE MACADAMS,
Lieut, C.A.M.C., Ontario Military Hospital,
Orpington, Kent.

SHE WILL WORK NOT ONLY FOR YOUR BEST INTERESTS BUT FOR THOSE OF YOUR WIVES, MOTHERS, SWEETHEARTS, SISTERS AND CHILDREN AFTER THE WAR.

Remember those who have helped you so nobly through the fight.

Poster for Roberta McAdams overseas election campaign, 1917

I never realised until my first campaign in 1921 what miserable incompetent creatures women were in the eyes of the public. I ought to have developed a terrible inferiority complex by the time it was over, for practically the only issue that seemed to concern the electorate or the opposition, was that I was a woman and worse an English woman....

> —*Irene Parlby*
> *"What Business Have Women In Politics?"*
> *Circa 1935*

It has been the dirtiest possible fight, but we won out with about 1,000 majority....

I feel that if I can help to smash this hideous party machine and free people from its yoke it will have been worth it. I feel as if I had been through rivers of mud and could never be clean again, or trust anyone again—

Some who had been pretending most to be our friends we found were traitors—and the venom of the Alix women—you could not believe—they were literally mad with spite! and the whole masonic bunch and the Institute worked like the devil against me, and no lie was too vile to be used....

> —*Irene Parlby*
> *Letter to Violet McNaughton*
> *July 22, 1921*

A man is no longer a novelty in the legislature and can get away with almost anything if he has been trained in the old political game but women are scarce and very new in these assemblies and there are always those waiting eagerly to point to their failures and longing for the day when they can enjoy themselves to the full in repeating "I told you so!"

> —*Irene Parlby*
> *Maclean's Magazine*
> *June 15, 1925*

My dear Mrs. Parlby:

I have been hearing rumors of your retirement from public life, which I hope are not true. I know you get very tired of it all, but we certainly do need you, and I hope you will continue.

It seems that the hostility to women in public life is not lessening; but rather growing, and as you have achieved a real place of influence, it will be a great loss to our forces if you should relinquish it....

> *With sincere affection*
> *Nellie L. McClung*

First meeting of newly-elected MLA's to name premier of United Farmers of Alberta government; Irene Parlby (seated left, front), circa 1921

VII Epilogue

In the decade after the War, it became obvious that women's suffrage would not bring about the millenium that the optimists had foretold. While their opponents had ranted about the ways in which voting would barbarize women, the suffragists had predicted that women might humanize society. They foresaw women working together to defeat self-serving governments, boycott partisan politics and clean up political graft. At a time when tens of thousands of prairie women were signing suffrage petitions and working for prohibition, this inspiring prospect seemed plausible enough. Women would march side by side, a shining sisterhood of reform.

As it happened, the suffrage movement *per se*, like most other mass crusades before and since, was relatively short-lived. The groups which had organized specifically to work for the vote, the equal franchise societies and political equality leagues, disbanded shortly after attaining their common goal. Here and there, attempts were made to sustain them as women's lobbies and as "schools in citizenship", but without much success. By the early twenties, the broadly based suffrage organizations had collapsed.

That is not to say that the aspirations of the suffragists were dead. There might not be a sisterhood, but there still could be reform. The initiative passed to the special interest groups, organizations like the National Council of Women, UFWA, and WCTU, which carried on the work, each from its own point of view. Among the issues which they took up were the by-now familiar "women's work" of education, medical services and child protection. There were new concerns like securing minimum wage laws, improving prison conditions, checking drug trafficking and fostering world peace. Some groups concentrated on encouraging women to run for public office, by finding suitable candidates and working on their campaigns. Others worked on problems like the shortage of domestic help and loopholes in women's property rights. A number were interested in the legalization of birth control and in the introduction of its more sinister step-sister, "eugenic" reform. (The advocates of "eugenics" called for the sterilization of "mental defectives", a loosely defined group of people whose characteristics included poverty, law-breaking and disease. These were thought by eugenicists to be linked to hereditary "feeble mindedness".)

Many of the issues take up the women's organizations during the twenties grew out of the same set of values as had inspired the suffrage campaign. While the movement continued to have some impact, its golden age of unity, growth and vigour was past. Young women were no longer attracted to it in great numbers: the image of women as motherly crusaders had lost its rallying power. The twenties was the decade of the "flapper", with her kneewagging dances and boozy good times. What effect did her image have on the prairie women? What was really going on in the everyday world of the time?

The answers to those questions are beyond the scope of this book. But there is one more episode from the twenties which deserves to be told here, as a postscript to "winning the vote". That is the Person's Case, the action initiated by five Albertans through which women became eligible to sit in the Senate.

The story really began in 1916, when Emily Murphy was appointed police magistrate for the city of Edmonton. On her first day in court, she was challenged by a defence lawyer who argued that her decisions were invalid because of her sex. His precedent was a decision of an English court in 1876: "women are persons in matters of pains and penalties, but are not persons in matters of right and privileges." Since being a magistrate was a privilege, Mrs. Murphy, a non-person, was ineligible. This taunt, the so-called "persons argument", was used repeatedly against both Judge Murphy and her Calgary colleague Alice Jamieson until 1917, when the provincial Supreme Court silenced it on the grounds of "reason and good sense."

Provoked by this experience, Judge Murphy did some research, and discovered that same troublesome word in Section 24 of the British North America Act, where Senate eligibility was restricted to "fit and qualified persons." Did it refer to women here? At Mrs. Murphy's instigation, a number of women's organizations asked the federal government to end the confusion by appointing a woman Senator. In 1921, a Montreal women's club went one step further and nominated a candidate—Judge Murphy. Their request was turned down for the familiar reason that in legal terms, "women are persons in matters of pains and penalties..."

Nothing further was accomplished until 1927, when Judge Murphy discovered that any five citizens could ask for an interpretation of the constitution. She quickly enlisted four other prestigious Albertans—Nellie McCLung, Henrietta Edwards, Louise McKinney and Irene Parlby—as co-signatories and sent the matter to the Supreme Court of Canada. "Does the word persons in Section 24 of the British North America Act, 1867, include female persons?" Nine months later, they received their answer. In a word, "no." It was not that women were not persons, the court decided. It was just that they, along with lunatics, criminals and children, had not been "fit and qualified" for Senate appointment in the eyes of the Fathers of Confederation. The remedy would be to amend the constitution.

Rather than wait for that to happen, Mrs. Murphy and her supporters appealed the case to the Privy Council in London, which at the time still had authority in Canada.

Here lawyers presented substantially the same arguments they had presented before the Supreme Court, but this time the decision was different. Privy Council noted that in some sections of the BNA Act "persons" clearly included both sexes, and in others the phrase "male persons" was used to refer to men only. In the clause describing the qualification of Senators, there was no specific mention of sex. Whatever the framers of the constitution had intended, there was nothing in the language of the Act to bar women from the Senate. As Nellie McClung wrote later, "It was so simple and so plain that we wondered now why we didn't think of it ourselves."

That was 1929. A year later, Liberal party worker Cairine Wilson of Ontario became Canada's first woman Senator, much to the disappointment of Judge Murphy who would have liked the honour herself. No prairie woman has yet been named to the Senate.

The next case [heard in my court] is also a breach of the Liquor Act. Before his client pleads, Counsel for the Defence gets to his feet and objects to my jurisdiction as a magistrate. On being requested to state his objection, he argues that I am not "a person" within the meaning of the Statutes. His argument takes up quite ten minutes and in the end is duly noted. Whereupon the hearing of the case proceeds.

On every subsequent case, this man, who is the most popular criminal lawyer in the city, persisted in raising the objection, while I persisted in hearing the whole argument, the thing appealing to my fancy immensely. Other barristers caught up the objection and we had a merry time of it. He was a poor fellow indeed, who could not put up a new aspect of the argument....

—*Emily Murphy*
Emily Murphy Crusader

October 25, 1917

E.E.A.H. Jackson Esq.
Messrs Cormack, MacKie & Van Allen,
Barristers, Edmonton

Sir,
I am informed this morning in the Women's Police Court at the conclusion of the case of Rex vs Nora Holt, you, in the presence of several persons made use of the following grossly insulting words—
"To Hell with Women Magistrates, this country is going to the dogs because of them, I would commit suicide before I would pass a sentence like that."
Unless I receive from you an unqualified apology in writing, I shall regretfully be obliged to henceforth refuse you admittance to this Court in the capacity of Counsel. I have the honour to be,

Sir,
Your obedient servant,
Emily Murphy
Police Magistrate for the
City of Edmonton

Judge Emily Murphy presiding in juvenile court, 1918

The Free Press says it isn't that women are wanting to get into the Senate in any overwhelming way. What irks them is that they are kept out.

—*Emily Murphy*
Letter to Nellie McClung
October 26, 1927

BNA ACT 1867-Section 24

"The Governor-General shall from Time to Time, in the Queen's Name, by Instrument under the Great Seal of Canada, summon qualified Persons *to the Senate; and, subject to the Provisions of this Act, every Person so summoned shall become and be a member of the Senate and a Senator."*

April 24, 1928
Supreme Court pronounced its judgement unanimously answering the question referred as follows:
"The question being understood to be: 'Are women eligible for appointment to the Senate of Canada', the Question is answered in the negative."

Reason:
Because Section 24 does not authorise the Governor-General to summon any persons to the Senate but only "qualified persons" and women were neither qualified by the common law or by the statutory provisions for the qualifications requisite for a Senator.

I hear...that it has been a terrible shock to the Eastern women that 5 coal-heavers and plough-pushers from Alberta (can anything good come out of Nazareth?) went over their heads to the Supreme Court without ever saying, "Please Ma'am can we do it?"

—*Emily Murphy*
Letter to Nellie McClung
December 2, 1927

*Emily
Murphy*

Dear ...[Nellie McClung]:
"Read your article re Argument of Persons. Admire your pluck but not your spirit. In thought, action and view you belong to the species of men closer than you do to women. The whole five of you. I seen your pictures."

[Nellie replies:]
The writer...has reduced us to nothing when he tells us he does not like our look!

To say that a woman is not beautiful has been considered damaging evidence against her and quite sufficient to offset her arguments.

I think these four women have beauty. Of course I may be prejudiced for I have known them long and love them well.

—*Nellie McClung*
Farm and Ranch Review
March 1, 1930

It took me 13 years and almost broke my heart but it was worth the fight.

—*Emily Murphy*
Letter to Mrs. Ginsberg in Palestine

This decision marks the abolition of sex in politics....Personally I do not care whether or not women ever sit in the senate, but we fought for the privilege for them to do so. We sought to establish the personal individuality of women and this decision is the announcement of our victory. It has been an up-hill fight.

—*Henrietta Muir Edwards*
Newspaper report
October 19, 1929

Dear Nellie:

You and I have been seeking pain, and maybe we have come to a time where we owe it to ourselves and our family not to seek it. If it comes we can't help it, but you see there is a distinction. I think, too, we might safely let ourselves to happiness a little more than we do. It isn't really wasting time for if we store up enough of it, it must just bubble out to others. —Anyway take care of yourself. Life would be dark, indeed, to many of us if anything were to happen to you.

—*Letter to Nellie McClung from Emily Murphy*

Henrietta
Muir Edwards

Women have been creatures of relationships, sex-relationships. She was someone's daughter, wife or mother. See what the Encyclopedia Brittanica has to say: "The very word 'woman' (old English *wifman*), etymologically meaning wife, sums up a long history of dependence and subordination from which the women of today have only gradually emancipated themselves in such parts of the world as come under Western civilization." Even yet, this question is eagerly asked about a woman who achieves distinction in any department of life: Who is she? Where is her man? What does he think of her activities?

Now that we are persons, I wonder if we will notice any difference. Will women cease to ask for confirmation of their stories or opinions from their nearest male relative?

Will women still give as an excuse, when they do not want to do something, "My husband will not let me!"

Will women ever grow to trust other women—will women doctors, dentists and lawyers receive their share of clients?

—Nellie McClung
Farm and Ranch Review

IT IS UP TO US!

It is a cold day for us poor women now, in Canada. We have the vote. We can sit in Parliament, on juries, on boards or commissions, or anywhere else where there are seats; and when there aren't any seats, we can have seats put in; and where the seats are hard, we can cushion them. Every door is open every bar is down; and now, though many things are wrong, we have no one to blame—and it is embarrassing!

It was so pleasant to be able to trace through our votelessness the cause of all social ills. We knew it was because we had no vote that a double standard of morals existed, unequal pay, unequal property rights. We traced it all back to our "political disability".

...Women have accomplished so much in the last few years that they have firmly established their humanity. They have become people. They are persons, not only 'in pains and penalties', but also 'in rights and privileges'.

The trench has been taken, but it has to be held, and that is sometimes the more difficult achievement. Sex prejudice is not dead. It is still hard for some to believe that those who are physically weaker may be equal in intelligence. But there will come, as a result of this new freedom for women, a great harvest of women writers. The long, long thoughts of many weary years will be set down as travellers who have climbed the hill rest upon the summit and discuss the devious and windy paths by which they have come. While they made the ascent, they naturally had not much to say. There will be books written from a new angle and a new method of reasoning, and surprising may be the conclusions reached. A new era is upon us in the world of literature!

216

European husband and wife

I like outspoken people, unpleasant though they may be. One of them came to me, and told me I was going to be defeated and why.

This is a man's town, she said. We don't want women messing around in public affairs. I have no confidence in women, won't even trust a woman to make my clothes, if I can get a man to do it.

I threw modesty to the winds, and asked her, if she could point to any man who had done any better than I had in public life. She said no—but then it wasn't natural. She said if I had stayed at home and conducted a salon and gathered around me the chosen spirits of the city, I could have done much more for my country.

I asked her, what she thought women had been created for, and she had the answer ready.

To bear children she said, and make homes. She said a woman should help her menfolk, instead of branching out into activities for herself.

Ladies Aids, I ventured and she agreed. Just that, she said, home-keeping hearts are happiest.

It has become increasingly apparent that the loyalty that existed among women when we were working for the vote has gone. Then, women could not be induced to slander each other. Now they can, easily—and the reason is not hard to see. In the struggle for the vote, all women stood to gain—and all therefore had an equal stake in the effort.

—*Nellie McClung*
Manuscript, personal papers

The first thing that should be done is to try and get men to believe that though they have lost a good, docile, capable servant, they have gained an understanding, intelligent friend and companion.

We must try to convince women that they must not expect both tips and wages; that if they claim equality, they must play fair; that they cannot make economic dependence, which no longer exists, an excuse for letting men pay their bills; that they must look for no favours or special privileges, but with dignity, courtesy and straightforwardness go in and possess the land, or at least their share of it.

—*Nellie McClung*
"Our Present Discontents"
Canadian Home Journal
March, 1929

Telephone operators

Sex prejudice and the male superiority complex, built up since time began, will not go out in one generation. And we, who have emerged from the shadows of the past, and are set free from many of its illusions, but are not yet received as members in full standing of the human family, chafe under some of its restrictions that are still laid upon us.

> —*Nellie McClung*
> *"Our Present Discontents"*
> Canadian Home Journal
> *March, 1929*

Our discontents are passing. We may yet live to see the day when women will be no longer news! And it cannot come too soon. I want to be a peaceful, happy, normal human being, pursuing my unimpeded way through life, never having to stop to explain, defend or apologize for my sex.

> —*Nellie McClung*
> *"A Retrospect"*
> The Country Guide
> *December 2, 1929*

The country is yours ladies; politics is simply public affairs. Yours & mine & everyone's. The government has enfranchised you, but it cannot emancipate you, that is done by your own processes of thought.

> —*Nellie McClung*
> The Calgary News-Telegram
> *1917*

Prairie woman, Lineham, Alberta, 1917

Biographies

Roberta Catherine MacAdams

B. Sarnia, Ontario, July 21, 1884; d. Dec., 1959. Graduated from the first class in Domestic Science at Macdonald Institute, Guelph, Ontario; did post-graduate work at University of Chicago. Came to Alberta in 1911; studied ways of organizing Women's Institutes in rural areas. In 1914, became supervisor of Domestic Science for Edmonton Public School System; established Home Economics departments in both elementary and high schools.

In 1916, enlisted in Canadian Army Medical Corps and was commissioned as Lieutenant. Posted to Ontario Military Hospital, Orpington, England, as a dietician. After enfranchisement of Alberta women, was encouraged by Beatrice Nasmyth, the only female Agent General in England, to run as a military candidate in the 1917 provincial election. (Servicemen overseas were a special constituency with two representatives.) Elected with 4,000 votes, 700 more than her closest rival. Sworn in on February 8, 1918, one of the first two women elected to a legislature in the British Empire. Was first woman to introduce a piece of legislation, a bill to incorporate the War Veterans' Next-Of-Kin Association.

Discharged from army in 1918; became organizer of Women's Program for Khaki University, a continuing education agency for servicemen. In 1919, appointed counsellor for war brides and homesteading wives under Soldier Settlement Board. Credited with convincing government to establish normal schools in Alberta.

Married in 1920 to Harvey S. Price; moved to Peace River country. Later retired to Calgary where she worked in Home and School.

Henrietta (Edwards) Muir

B. Montreal, Quebec, Dec. 19, 1849; d. 1931. Born into a wealthy family; educated in Canada, Europe and USA. Acclaimed painter of florals and miniatures. In 1875, organized the Working Girls' Association in Montreal, with a 60-room boarding house. It also provided vocational courses and an employment bureau. Published first women's magazine in Canada, *Women's Work In Canada*, printing it herself.

In 1876, married Dr. Oliver C. Edwards; moved to Fort Qu'Appelle, Saskatchewan in 1883, and to Ottawa in 1890. Here she helped Lady Aberdeen found the National Council of Women and the Victorian Order of Nurses. In 1903, moved to Fort Macleod, Alberta. Compiled a handbook on the legal status of women in Alberta. Book on legal status of women in Canada published by federal government in 1924. For many years, convenor of laws for the National Council of Women; also president of the Alberta Provincial Council. Widely respected for her precise legal mind and comprehensive knowledge of laws relating to women.

Sarah Katherine (McEwen) Ramsland

B. Minnesota, USA, July 19, 1882; d. Prince Albert, Saskatchewan, April 4, 1967. Daughter of a member of the Minnesota Legislature. Trained at St. Cloud, Minnesota Teachers' College; taught in Minnesota before marrying Magnus O. Ramsland, a real estate broker. Moved to Buchanan, Saskatchewan, in 1906, where her three children were born, and to Kamsack, Saskatchewan, in 1913. In 1917, her husband was elected to provincial legislature as Liberal member for Pelly River constituency. When he died in 1918, she won ensuing by-election, the first woman elected to Saskatchewan Assembly; campaign was rancorous, with little support for Mrs. Ramsland from provincial party. Interested in temperance and education, especially high schools for rural areas. Moved to Regina in 1920. Re-elected in 1921, but defeated by a Progressive in 1925. Worked for Saskatchewan Provincial Library, organizing and running travelling library service. Remarried in 1942 to W.G.F. Scythes of Regina.

Emily (Ferguson) Murphy

B. Simcoe County, Ontario, March, 1868; d. Edmonton, Alberta, Oct. 9, 1933. Educated in Ontario; married to Rev. Arthur Murphy in 1887, and spent next 16 years as clergyman's wife, moving from rectory to rectory and raising her daughters. Moved west to Swan River, Manitoba, in 1904. She was now free to write full time. In 1907, she moved to Edmonton. Three books, *Janey Canuck In The West*, based on life in Swan River, *Open Trails* and *Seeds of Pine,* about her travels in Alberta, were published in 1910, 1912, and 1914 respectively.

Influenced by the women she met in rural Alberta, she worked with the local Council of Women to secure Dower Act in 1910. Joined or organized numerous women's clubs, including Canadian Women's Press Club, Federated Women's Institutes, Women's Canadian Club. Worked to save Old Fort Edmonton from destruction; exposed mismanagement of Edmonton Hospital; advocated registration of women for war work; sought a "Children's Protection Act". In 1913, was a founding member of Edmonton Equal Franchise League; worked on petition campaigns and delegations. Decorated by the King, 1915.

In 1916, appointed police magistrate in Edmonton, the first woman in Canada to preside over a Women's Court. Like Alice Jamieson in Calgary, was snubbed and opposed, but perservered. "The Black Candle", her comprehensive report on the drug trade in Canada, published in 1922. Worked for rehabilitation of women she sentenced, sterilization of the insane, treatment for TB, and child welfare laws.

In 1927, initiated the "Person's Case", partly because she wanted to be a senator. After the case was won, she was passed over for political reasons.

Alice Jamieson

B.?; d. 1949; came to Calgary in 1902 with her husband R.R.Jamieson; became involved in community work. In 1912, helped to found local Council of Women; was president for six years. With Henrietta Edwards and others, was very active in women's suffrage work, addressing the legislature, interviewing the Premier, and presenting petitions to the government. Later, supported women running for office.

In 1913, appointed Magistrate of Juvenile Court in Calgary, the first woman in any judiciary in the British Empire. In 1916, appointed Police Magistrate to hear women's cases. "Being the first woman magistrate was no position to excite envy," she later told a reporter. "I had to fight down a good deal of prejudice on the part of certain members of the legal profession and the police department.

"When I first assumed my duties in the police court, with cold shoulders greeting me on every hand, I said to myself, 'I don't know why I ever came here—I don't have to do this,' and then I drew myself up and said, 'Well, I'm here—and I'm here to stay!' " When she was challenged on the grounds that women were not legally persons, the Alberta Supreme Court upheld her authority. Retired in 1932.

Louise (Crummy) McKinney

B. Frankville, Ontario, Sept. 22, 1868; d. Claresholm, Alberta, 1931. Trained as a teacher, although she wanted to be a doctor. ("Even as a child " she said, "I recognized and resented the disabilities laid upon women.") Worked as WCTU organizer in the United States; married prohibitionist James McKinney in 1894. They had one child, a son. Moved to Claresholm in 1903, where she helped organize the WCTU. Was provincial president and Dominion vice-president, holding each office for more than twenty years. Also held the offices of world vice-president in both the WCTU and the IODE.

Elected to Alberta Legislature as non-partisan league candidate, 1917. With Roberta MacAdams, was pioneer woman MLA. Supported aid for immigrants the retarded, widows and deserted wives; advocated strict enforcement of liquor control laws. Introduced a Dower Law drafted by herself and Henrietta Muir Edwards. Called herself "domestic" but added "my life has never been bounded by the four walls of a home. I have always been interested in affairs of church and state". The only woman to sign the basis of union founding the United Church of Canada, 1925.

Nellie Letitia (Mooney) McClung

B. Grey County, Ontario, Oct. 20, 1873; d. Victoria, British Columbia, 1951. As a child, moved with family to farm near Brandon, Manitoba. Started school at age 10; held teaching certificate at 15; taught at Manitou, Manitoba. In 1896, married Robert Wesley McClung, son of temperance worker and suffragist, Mrs. J.W. McClung. Encouraged by her mother-in-law, wrote best-selling novel *Sowing Seeds in Danny* (1908), the first of 16 books. Bore five children, four sons and a daughter.

In 1911, moved to Winnipeg. Active in WCTU and Canadian Women's Press Club. A founding member and leading spirit of the Manitoba Political Equality League in 1912. For two years lectured extensively for the League in Manitoba; also lectured elsewhere in Canada, in Britain and the USA. "Starred" in the famous mock parliament of 1914.

Later that year, moved to Edmonton because of husband's work; joined Edmonton Equal Franchise League, and once again took a leading role in suffrage work. In 1921, elected as Liberal member in Alberta Legislature, but confessed to being a poor party member, because too independent. Worked for mothers' allowances, public health nurses, free medical and dental care for children, liberalized birth control and divorce laws and improved property rights for married women.

Defeated by 60 votes in 1926 because of her strong stand on prohibition. Turned to writing full time. In 1928, was one of the signatories in the "Person's Case". Retired to Victoria in 1933. On CBC Board of Governors 1933-42. Canadian delegate to the League of Nations, 1938.

Dr. Amelia Yeomans

B. Quebec, March 29, 1842; d. Calgary, Alberta, 1913. Widow; graduated from Ann Arbour, Michigan, School of Medicine and began her practice in Winnipeg with her daughter, Dr. Lilian Yeomans. Spoke out frankly on venereal disease, "white slavery", alcohol abuse. A leader in the Women's Christian Temperance Union; founded the Manitoba Equal Suffrage Society in 1894. Its motto— "peace on earth, good will towards men". One of the first people to draw attention to the problems of non-English speaking settlers. Moved to Calgary in 1905; became vice-president of the national WCTU, honorary vice-president of the Ottawa Equal Suffrage Society and honorary president of the Calgary Suffrage Association.

Mary Irene (Marryatt) Parlby

B. London, England, Jan. 9, 1868; d. 1965. Daughter of a well-to-do army officer. Brought up in England and India. Given a gentlewoman's education in literature, music and languages. Came to Canada in 1896 to visit friends. In 1897, married Oxford graduate and Alberta homesteader Walter Parlby of Alix. Their only child, a son, born 1899. Worked solely as a housewife until 1913, when she was elected secretary of the newly formed Alix Country Women's Club. In 1916, elected first president of the United Farm Women of Alberta; worked for women's suffrage, municipal hospitals, public health nurses; travelled through province organizing local clubs. Found the work difficult and discouraging. In 1920, retired from UFWA executive; at that time wrote to tell Violet McNaughton, "home is where I really belong and *not* in public life. Am too lazy mentally."

In 1921, elected to Alberta Legislature and appointed minister without portfolio. Assigned herself special responsiblity for women's rights. Worked for an enlarged public health service, educational reform, travelling medical clinics, sexual sterilization of mental defectives, and improved property rights for married women.

In 1928, co-operated with Emily Murphy in the action to open Canadian Senate to women. In 1930, one of three Canadian delegates to the League of Nations. In 1935, retired from public life due to ill health. Continued to write for radio and magazines, including a regular gardening column for the Grain Growers' Guide.

Violet Clara (Jackson) McNaughton

B. Borden, Kent, England, Nov. 11, 1879; d. Saskatoon, Saskatchewan, Feb. 3, 1968. Educated in private schools; did social work for two years in big city slums; taught for several years. Applied to British civil service but was rejected because she was one half inch short of the 5 foot minimum height requirement.

Joined her father and brother on Saskatchewan homestead in 1909. Married neighbour John McNaughton in 1910 and through him became involved in local Grain Growers' Association. In 1913, elected first woman delegate to a provincial GGA Convention; with Francis Beynon and F.W.Green of the Grain Growers, helped plan a farm women's meeting that year. Named secretary of organizing committee for women's association. Elected first president of the Women Grain Growers in 1914; worked hard for women's suffrage, improved rural medical care, fairer property laws for wives, co-operative marketing, and the streamlining of housekeeping; wrote a column for *Saturday Press* and *Prairie Farmer,* 1916-17.

Resigned from WGGA Executive in 1917; in 1918 became president of the Interprovincial Council of Farm Women, an alliance of the three prairie farm women's associations. First woman elected to SGGA board of directors; also first president women's section of the Canadian Council of Agriculture, and in that capacity helped draft platform of the progressive movement which swept Canada in the 1921 federal election. From 1925-1950, editor of "Mainly for Women" page in the *Western Producer*.

Especially recognized for her role in settlement of long-standing feud in the farm movement, 1926. Attended Prague congress of the Women's International League for Peace and Freedom, 1929. After resignation from the *Western Producer* wrote weekly column, "Jottings By The Way". Made Honorary Doctor of Laws by the University of Saskatchewan, 1951.

Lillian (Beynon) Thomas

B. ?; d. Winnipeg, Manitoba, 1961. Moved to Manitoba in 1889; graduated from the University of Manitoba with a BA in 1905. Taught for a few months before joining the staff of the *Free Press*. Wrote under the name of "Lillian Laurie". In 1910, worked for the University of Saskatchewan, organizing Homemakers'

Clubs in the south of the province. Married A. Vernon Thomas, 1911. Helped found Manitoba Political Equality League, 1912. Worked in New York as a journalist for five years after World War I. Returned to Canada as a free-lance writer. Published works include short stories, a novel and two plays.

Ella Cora Hind

B. Toronto, Ontario, 1861; d. Winnipeg, Oct. 6, 1942. Orphaned as a youngster; brought up by grandfather and Aunt Alice Hind on a farm in Ontario. Partially completed teacher training before coming to Winnipeg with her aunt in 1882. Turned down by *The Manitoba Free Press* because of her sex, she taught herself to type on one of first machines in the West. Worked for a law office until 1893 when she opened a public stenography bureau on borrowed money. Contributed agricultural reports to the *Free Press,* business articles to American commercial publications in the United States. Did stenographic work for local agricultural organizations. In 1898, made her first crop survey and harvest prediction for Maclean Publications in Toronto.

In 1901, finally hired by *Free Press* as an agricultural reporter. In 1904 began series of 29 annual harvest predictions which won her a world-wide reputation and helped determine the price paid for Canadian wheat. As agricultural editor, developed first paper devoted to farming as a business. Especially interested in livestock breeding, expansion of export markets and construction of a northern sea port.

Honoured by Western Canadian Livestock Union, Co-operative Wool Growers, United Grain Growers, Winnipeg Grain Exchange, Canadian Society of Technical Agriculturists, Manitoba Dairy Association and University of Manitoba for her contributions to prairie agriculture. At 74, took a 27-country world tour, examining farm practices.

Meanwhile, had joined the WCTU. Leading member of Dr. Amelia Yeoman's Manitoba Equal Franchise Club. In later years, very active in the Manitoba Political Equality League, which ran the successful suffrage campaign in Manitoba.

Timeline

1682 Henry Kelsey, the first white man to visit western Canada, returns to Fort York with an Indian wife.

1714 Working on behalf of the Hudson Bay Company traders at York Factory, Thanadelthur, better known to history as the Slave Woman, and her party trek across the barrens as ambassadors to her people, the Dene. Her mission is to make peace between the Cree and Chipewyans, and encourage the latter to come to the Bay.

1803 Disguised as a man, Mary Fubbester (the "Orkney Lass"), starts work as a clerk in a Hudson Bay Co. fur trade post somewhere in Rupert's Land, a job which is not open to European women. She is forced to quit in 1807, because she has a baby.

1806 Marie-Anne Lagimodière accompanies her fur trader husband on to the prairies. She is the first Canadian woman to settle in the West. Her daughter Reine, born in 1807 at Pembina River House, is probably the first white child born west of the Great Lakes. Marie-Anne's grandson is Louis Riel.

1812 The first agricultural settlers in the West arrive at Lord Selkirk's Red River Colony.

1844 Four Grey Nuns leave their motherhouse in Montreal to travel by birch bark canoe to the Red River Colony. They are the first nursing order in the West. In 1860, others of their order extend nursing service into Saskatchewan, establishing a hospital and dispensary at Ile-à-la Crosse, 200 miles north west of Prince Albert. In 1863, yet another small group open a hospital at Father Lacombe's St. Albert (Alberta) mission. Later a small number of secular women will arrive to do similar work as missionaries: for example Onesime Dorval who joined Father Lacombe in 1877 and Lucy Baker who went to Prince Albert in 1878. Both are teachers.

1870 First Riel Rebellion.

Following the Rebellion, the Hudson Bay Company's fur trade territory *(Rupert's Land) is transferred to Canada.* This includes all the land between the three-year old Dominion and the Crown Colony of British Columbia. *Under the Manitoba Act, the old Red River settlement is admitted to Confederation as a province.* The rest of the area, which includes most of present-day Alberta, British Columbia and Manitoba, become part of the North-West Territories.

1871 *The population of the prairies is about 25,000.*

Under Manitoba's "Act Respecting Married Women", any property a wife holds in her own name is free from her husband's control and debts, but her earnings are his, unless he is cruel, insane, drunken, or neglectful, in which case the court entitles her to her earnings and those of her dependent children. (In 1975 revision of this Act is enacted as The Married Woman's Act of Manitoba.)

1875 Inspired by the appeal of missionary Rev. George McDougall, Ontario school teacher Elizabeth Barrett journeys to what is now Alberta by wagon, York boat and "prairie schooner" to work first at Whitefish Lake and later at Morley. In 1878, she and Gussie McDougall open a Methodist mission and school at Fort Macleod. (McDougall's own wife Eliza was the real pioneer, coming out with 7 children in 1862.)

Under c. 49, s. 48-53 of the Revised Statutes of Canada, a married woman in the North-West Territories may exercise the same freedom in managing her own property, earnings and business debts as if she were single, but she is not responsible for household debts or her own support. The principle of a wife's independence in business dealings is reaffirmed by the Married Women's Property Ordinance of 1889 and by later provincial Acts.

1877 A first (but hollow) recognition of the legal capabilities of women in Alberta comes in 1877 when Mary Drever Macleod, Julia Winder, Julia Shurtliff, Annie McDougall and Eliza Hardisty (wives of three police officers, a missionary and a trader respectively) sign as witness to Treaty No. 7 with the Blackfoot.

1880 Chapter 39 of the Consolidated Statutes of Manitoba states that "as a rule the father shall have custody and control of his infant children". If the father bars the mother from seeing her children, she can appeal to the court which *may* grant her access. The father can appoint a guardian as he sees fit, although the court may grant the mother custody *if* the father is dead—providing of course that she hasn't committed adultery in which case she forfeits her children. As long as the father lives, he may dispose of his children at will. (See entries under 1890 for similar laws in the Territories.)

1881 The first woman licenced to practice medicine in Western Canada, Dr. Charlotte Ross, arrives in the frontier town of Whitemouth, Manitoba intending to care only for her own family, but is increasingly called on as the community doctor. Other notable pioneer doctors were Amelia and Lilian Yeomans, mother and daughter, who specialized in midwifery, gynecology and pediatrics, beginning in 1882 and 1885 respectively. Both were Winnipeg suffragists.

1885 *The Canadian Pacific Railway is completed from East to West.*

Under a Territorial ordinance, unmarried women property holders are entitled to vote and hold office in school matters, but married women with property are excluded until 1888.

The Manitoba Real Property Act stipulates that when a woman property owner marries she must get a new certificate of title bearing her husband's name. Alberta makes a similar requirement in 1906.

Under the Devolution of Estates Act, a wife's right to a share of her husband's estate ("*dower*"), which is recognized by British common law and Canadian statutes, *is abolished* in Manitoba. The Territories Real Property Act disallows dower elsewhere on the prairies after 1887.

For the third year in a row, Sir John A. Macdonald introduces a franchise bill which would give the vote to unmarried women who meet certain property qualifications. After being ignored for two years running, the provision this time provokes *seven* days of fatuous debate before it is soundly defeated. One biographer suggests that Macdonald favoured woman suffrage because he expected women to be tradition-loving conservatives.

Second North West Rebellion.

During the second North-West Rebellion, Mother Hannah Grier of the Anglican Order of St. John the Divine and her staff of graduate nurses answer a plea for emergency care on the battlefields. They and other nurses set up temporary hospitals under primitive conditions.

1886 W.C.T.U. founder Letitia Youmans visits the West as a movement organizer. She appoints Mrs. W.W. Andrews as territorial superintendent.

1887 In Manitoba, women taxpayers, both married and single, are allowed to vote in municipal elections, but they will not be made eligible for municipal office until 1917.

1889 Mary Ellen Birtles, one of three in the first graduating class of the Winnipeg General Hospital school of nursing, starts work in the new two-nurse hospital at Medicine Hat, the only one between Nanaimo and Winnipeg. Later, she will be the first head nurse at Brandon (1892) and Calgary (1894). In her first hospitals, the nurses did the job of orderly, cook and wardmaid.

1890 Sometime around this date, *Icelandic women in Manitoba found the prairie's first women's suffrage association,* under the leadership of Mrs. M.J. Benedictson.

The school franchise and the right to hold office is extended to women ratepayers in Manitoba.

Under the laws of the N.W.T. (Consolidated Ordinances, chapter 21) only male British subjects may serve as jurors. This is also the law in Manitoba.

Chapter 21 of the Ordinances rules that a father shall be the sole guardian of any children under 14, except in unusual situations where the court has to intervene. A woman who commits adultery has no legal right to even see her children. A man is not similarly disbarred from fatherhood.

1891 *The population of the prairies has reached about 250,000.*

1893 In addition to petitioning the Manitoba government for political rights regardless of sex, the W.C.T.U. stages a "mock parliament" in Winnipeg with Dr. Amelia Yeomans as premier and speakers gravely debate the pros and cons of the issue.

1894 Stung by the fate of Manitoba's first suffrage bill, Dr. Amelia Yeomans, Cora Hind and other W.C.T.U. members organize the Manitoba Equal Franchise Club, the first anglophone suffrage association in the West. Men may be members but not elected officers.

In the Territories, unmarried women are permitted to vote in municipal elections, but they cannot hold office.

1895 In Regina, Catherine Simpson-Hayes publishes *Prairie Pot Pourri,* probably the first book written on and about the prairies. She will also write the prairies' first play and song.

Nicholas Flood Davin of Regina, Conservative MP (and lover of feminist Catherine Simpson-Hayes) proposes women's suffrage in the federal House. He draws three days of inflated discussion and a 2-to-1 "no" vote.

Lady Ishbel Aberdeen, wife of the Governor-General, who two years before had founded the National Council of Women, initiates a Local Council of Edmonton, one of the stops on her western tour.

1898 The task of determining who is eligible to vote passes from federal to provincial jurisdiction.

Mission doctor Elizabeth Matheson begins her wilderness practice at Onion Lake, Saskatchewan.

The same year that four members of the Victorian Order of Nurses go to work in the Klondike, Lily E. Bristow of the V.O.N. arrives in Regina to run single-handed, the cottage hospital established by the Local Council of Women which in time will become the Regina General. In 1901, she establishes a training school.

1899 Catherine Simpson-Hayes, the West's pioneer woman journalist, joins the staff of the *Winnipeg Free Press,* where she will edit the first page for prairie women. From the amount of mail she receives, she concludes that the page "filled a crying need" for lonely farm women.

Among the women who will later enter the profession are (1) Ethel Heydon Davidson who worked in Calgary in the nineteen teens under the pen name "Alberta West". Her first employers in Alberta had expected a man, but she got the job anyway. She was a suffragist. (2) Gertrude Watt, better know as "Peggy" was women's editor and columnist for the *Edmonton Saturday News,* and founder of the Edmonton Chapter of the Canadian Women's Press Club (1908). (3) Kennethe M. Haig was an editorial writer for the *Winnipeg Free Press* and the biographer of E. Cora Hind. (4) Katherine Hughes, on staff with the *Edmonton Bulletin* from 1906 to 1908 was the first provincial archivist for Alberta.

1900 The Married Women's Property Act in Manitoba makes a wife responsible for her own property, wages, profits, etc., and empowers her to manage it as freely as if she were unmarried. She is also jointly responsible for the support of her children.

The Married Women's Protection Act in Manitoba permits the wife of a cruel, drunken or irresponsible husband to ask for a court order freeing her from obligation to live with him, barring him from her residence, awarding her custody of their children and requiring him to pay support and court costs. In 1912, similar provisions were enacted in the tighter, tougher Wives' and Children's Maintenance Act.

1901 E. Cora Hind is hired by the *Winnipeg Free Press* as a marketing and agricultural reporter. In time she becomes the paper's agricultural editor and an internationally respected expert on grain growing and livestock production. Her successor will be Miriam Green Ellis of the *Family Herald* and *Eastern Star.*

1902 Under Cap. 48s. 4 of the Revised Statues of Manitoba, the widow of an intestate is entitled to one third of the estate if she has children and the entire estate if she doesn't. There is no such guarantee if the husband has made a will.

1905 *Alberta and Saskatchewan attain provincial status.* By now, Manitoba includes the area around Lakes Winnipeg and Winnipegosis. The remainder of the present-day province is still in the Territories.

1906 Calgary-born violinist Kathleen Parlow begins her professional career with a very successful European tour.

The founding convention of a national Canadian Women's Press Club (quickly dubbed Cats With Pointed Claws by those who object to professional associations for women) is held in Winnipeg. Catherine Simpson-Hayes is elected president.

The Municipal Act in Manitoba is amended so that only "men, unmarried women or widows" with property can vote in municipal elections, rather than "male or female" ratepayers who had been eligible earlier. Married women's voting rights are restored in 1907 due to public protest.

1908 A party led by Mary Schaeffer, later Mrs. Warren of Banff, "discovers" Maligne Lake in what is now Jasper National Park.

1909 At a joint convention the Alberta and Saskatchewan provincial W.C.T.U. pledges to work more actively for women's suffrage.

1910 *The organization of government-sponsored Homemakers' Clubs is begun in Saskatchewan by Lillian Thomas.* The first provincial convention is held in January, 1911.

A Women's Labor League dedicated to women's suffrage is formed in Winnipeg.

In Alberta, the Married Woman's Relief Act empowers the court to grant an allowance from her husband's estate to a widow who, in the opinion of the court, received less from her husband's will than she would have had he died intestate, but leaves the amount of the settlement up to the court. In 1920, a spouse will be guaranteed from 33% to 100% of his or her partner's estate under The Intestate Succession Act.

1911 *The population of the prairies has mushroomed to about 1,300,000.*

The Saskatchewan Deserted Wives' Maintenance Act empowers the courts to require husbands to pay support if they desert their wives or force them to leave due to cruelty.

The Grain Growers' Association of Manitoba officially declares their support for "votes for women".

The Trades and Labor Council in Regina declares its support of women's suffrage and equal pay for equal work.

On a cross-Canada speaking tour, British suffragette Emmeline Pankhurst stops at Winnipeg and Victoria. Her Winnipeg address is reprinted in the *Grain Growers' Guide,* but it does not provoke much comment.

1912 The Saskatchewan Grain Growers' Association affirms that women should be allowed to vote, but they reject a resolution calling for the opening of homesteads to wives and spinsters.

In Manitoba the Illegitimate Children's Act provides that an unwed mother could bring court action against the alleged father. If her claims were substantiated in court, he can be ordered to pay expenses and support.

In Alberta, The Rural Municipality Act, The Town Act and The Village Act (1913) empower any ratepayer to vote but restrict office-holding to men.

The United Farmers of Alberta endorse women's suffrage.

Suffragist and feminist Francis Beynon begins a four-year stint as women's editor of the *Grain Growers' Guide.* Until she quits in 1917, she will use her position as a tool for organizing women around "feminist" issues.

Convinced by experience of their inability to improve factory conditions by working indirectly through politicians, a group of Winnipeg writers decide they would have more clout as voters. On April 9, they found the *Manitoba Political Equality League* under president Lillian Thomas. It is to have a short (1912-1917) but fiery career.

Under a new Saskatchewan law, the father of an illegitimate child can be ordered to pay support if paternity can be established. A similar law, the Children of Unmarried Parents Act, is passed in Alberta in 1923.

Saskatchewan passes an act prohibiting white women from working for any "Japanese, Chinaman or other Oriental person". Manitoba passes a similar act in 1913.

In a Regina lecture British suffragette Barbara Wylie urges Canadian women to action, but doesn't get much response, although she may have inspired MLA Bradshaw to bring the subject up in the Saskatchewan Assembly a few days later.

In the Saskatchewan Legislature, J.E. Bradshaw introduces the first of several unsuccessful suffrage measures, all of which are defeated on the ground that women are disinterested in politics.

1913 Thanks to speeches by Nellie McClung, Lillian Thomas, Cora Hind and Mae Clendennan, a first farm women's convention in Saskatchewan turns into a suffrage rally. The women vote to retain full membership in the Grain Growers', but also to organize an affiliated but independent society of their own.

Although the Alberta Infants Act stipulates that "the father of an infant...from time to time as he may think fit may dispose of the custody and education" of his children, the mother is permitted to be guaranteed some guardianship rights after the father's death.

Members of the Manitoba Political Equality League are heckled by passers-by as they hand out literature and collect signatures for a suffrage petition at the Winnipeg summer stampede. Afterwards, Francis Beynon reports, "I am ashamed to have to say it, but the rudeness of women has helped to win the sympathy of many men".

After what is generally understood as a promise from the premier of Saskatchewan to extend political rights to women as soon as they show an interest, women working on their own initiative, but with the assistance of the Grain Growers' Association, send in 2,500 names on petitions. By far the longest, (157 names) comes from the little town of Moosomin. The Premier is not persuaded to act.

An Equal Suffrage League is formed in Edmonton with Dr. W.H. Alexander, a university professor, as president.

1914 *World War I.*

One of the first people to see the potential of co-operation between men and women as members with equal standing in the farm movement, Violet McNaughton of Harris, Saskatchewan, is elected first president of the *Women Grain Growers.* (A year earlier, she had been the first female delegate to a Grain Growers Convention.) Zoa Haight is vice-president and Erma Stocking, secretary. After the 1914 convention, Francis Beynon wrote, "The women who attended...were so radical that nothing less free than the W.G.G.A. could have contained them".

With the help of Francis Beynon, the first political equality league in Saskatchewan is formed at Moosomin on February 27.

In March the Manitoba Liberal party write women's suffrage into their election platform. They decide that a Liberal government would still require a substantial petition before making the change.

Turning the anti-woman-suffrage lectures of the Manitoba premier to good advantage, the Manitoba Political Equality League stage a crowd-pleasing "mock parliament" with Nellie McClung in a merciless parody of Sir Rodmond Roblin.

When the U.F.A. opens its membership to women at its annual convention, those farm women present hold a spur-of-the-moment meeting. Although no permanent organization is formed, the women go home to organize the local clubs which banded together as a U.F.A. Women's Auxiliary in 1915. In 1916, the independent U.F.W.A. is formed with Irene Parlby as president.

Alice Jamieson, a prominent Calgary clubwoman and community worker, is appointed judge of the juvenile court in Calgary. She will subsequently give leadership in the Alberta suffrage campaign through the Calgary Local Council of Women which she helped to found.

On October 9, the Edmonton Equal Franchise League and the Calgary Local Council of Women present a petition to the government on behalf of 12,000 signers and 44 associations.

1915 Under the Alberta Married Woman's Home Protection Act, a wife can prevent any transaction involving her homesite. A more workable revision of this law will be passed as *The Dower Act* of 1917. It is amended in 1918 and 1919, but not significantly changed until 1926 when a wife gains a life interest in some of her husband's personal property.

The Edmonton Grads, a world-famous women's basketball team, begin their career in high school competitions. For twenty-five years, they ruled the courts, winning 502 of their 522 games, including all the exhibition matches held at four Olympic Games. (Basketball was not an official event.)

Nellie McClung publishes *In Times Like These,* a rousing collection of feminist and pacifist essays.

The laws governing municipal politics in Saskatchewan are standardized so that all women, regardless of marital status, can participate as electors and candidates.

In February a large delegation representing the U.F.A., Edmonton Equal Franchise League, Calgary Local Council and National Council of Women appeal to their Alberta government to include women in a liquor referendum, but without success.

The first meeting of the Saskatchewan Provincial Equal Franchise Board is called by Violet McNaughton. It is intended to co-ordinate publicity and educational work throughout the province. Mrs. F.A. Lawton of Yorkton is elected president; Mrs. S.N. Haight of Keeler, vice-president, and Miss S.A. Van Alstyne of Moosomin, secretary.

Within weeks of its formation, the Provincial Equal Franchise Board arranges a delegation of 100 to present a 10,000 name suffrage petition to the Saskatchewan government.

Offered half-price memberships in the Manitoba Grain Growers' Association, farm women sign up on the condition of equal rights for all.

On December 23, suffragists present the new Liberal premier of Saskatchewan with a petition bearing 43,000 names, two and a half times the minimum number set by the government.

In a letter to the president of the United Farmers, the premier of Alberta declares his intention to admit women to full political equality with men.

1916 On January 27, less than two weeks after its introduction into the house, the *Manitoba Equal Suffrage Measure* receives third reading, amid noisy rejoicing from the galleries. Thanks to last-minute lobbying by members of the P.E.L., the right to hold office is also extended to women.

Addressing a strong suffrage delegation to the Legislative Assembly, Scott of *Saskatchewan* commits his government to immediate action on *women's suffrage.* It is Valentine's Day, which shows how the government feels about it; the women take it more seriously. Despite the sparse population, inconvenient transportation and bad weather, the movement had gathered signatures of another 10,000 supporters. The bill received royal assent on *March 14.*

On *April 19,* women gang into the galleries of the Legislature building in Edmonton to hear third reading of measures to enfranchise them. The *Alberta Equal Suffrage Act* gives women "absolute equality" with men in provincial, municipal and school affairs.

Saskatchewan suffrage leaders and Nellie McClung try unsuccessfully to find allies for an organized assault on federal election laws—because prairie women still have no direct voice in dominion politics.

When the Borden government defeats an amendment which would have extended the federal franchise to those women with provincial political rights, the Women's Institutes of Alberta and the Women's Industrial Association of Edmonton demand to know where the government stands, but they aren't told.

Responding to requests from women's organizations that a female judge hear women's cases, the Alberta government appoints Emily Murphy and Alice Jamieson as police magistrates in Edmonton and Calgary respectively. Their authority is immediately challenged on the grounds they are not legally "persons".

Under the Mothers' Allowances Act, a poor mother in Manitoba could receive a government grant if her children were "neglected" because of the death, insanity, imprisonment or disability of their father.

Amendments to the Manitoba Shop Regulation Act regulate the working hours and conditions of women and children in retail or wholesale businesses. For example, women cannot work longer than 14 hours per day, 60 hours per week, and they must have a place to sit down when they are not busy.

1917 After working for several years with neglected children, Jean Ethel MacLachlan is named juvenile court judge for Saskatchewan; her work will earn her national recognition within her profession.

Louise C. McKinney of the Non-Partisan League and *Roberta MacAdams,* a soldiers' representative, are elected to the Alberta Legislature. They are the *first female members of any House in Canada or the British Empire.*

The Alberta Dower Act is passed (see 1915).

In Alberta, wives, daughters and sisters of male ratepayers, as well as all ratepayers regardless of sex or marital status, are allowed to participate in school politics. (However husbands, sons and brothers of female ratepayers are not included.)

The Military Voters Act extends the federal franchise to all military personnel, which incidentally includes nurses.

In an effort to win re-election despite the conscription issue, Borden alters the electorate by excluding conscientious objectors and some recent immigrants, and by adding the immediate female relatives of servicemen. The *Wartime Elections Act* is to be in force until the war ends.

1918 In Kamsack, Saskatchewan, Sarah Katherine Ramsland is elected to complete the term of her husband who had died during the post-war flu epidemic. Just before her defeat in 1925, she will introduce a resolution urging the equalization of the grounds of divorce for men and women.

Despite bitter opposition from French-Canadian MPs, a bill giving the federal franchise—but not the right to hold office—to Canadian women receives third reading on April 12. Women's war service figures largely in the pro-suffrage arguments. The right to hold office is added in 1919.

Senator L.O. David moves that unmarried women under 30 should be disenfranchised because they are innocent maidens who should spend all their time "preparing themselves to fulfill the duties of their noble mission". Of 52 votes cast, 19 support David.

For the first time, female delegates are admitted to the convention of the Alberta Federation of Labour.

At the annual meeting of the Provincial Equal Franchise Board in Saskatoon members resolve to ask the government for a minimum wage of $12 per week for women and girls. This is one of the P.E.F.B.'s last meetings.

A Women's Party organized in the East to "unite women of the nation for their political responsibilities" does not appeal to farm movement people like Violet McNaughton who prefer the ideal of co-operation between the sexes.

The Minimum Wage Act in Manitoba establishes a board with jurisdiction over working conditions, hours, and pay of women in shops, mail order houses and factories in the cities.

The *Dower Act in Manitoba* gives wives the right to veto any transaction involving their "homestead", their home and up to 6 city lots or one-half section of land, even after the death of their husbands. In addition, they are guaranteed one-third of the total estate regardless of what their husband's wills stipulate. The 1919 revision of the Act is more precisely worded but the same in substance.

1919 Under the Naturalization Act, a British subject who married an "alien" was permitted to retain her citizenship. Previously, the wife automatically took her husband's nationality, and thus lost her citizenship rights.

In Alberta, the Municipal Hospitals Act, as drafted by a committee convened by Irene Parlby of the U.F.W.A. is passed. The U.F.W.A. also "drew up the plans" for travelling clinics and public health nursing in Alberta.

In Alberta, mothers whose husbands are dead or insane may apply for relief under the Mothers' Allowances Act. The program is extended to the wives of cripples or invalids in 1926.

Women, and women only, are covered by a *minimum wage law* in Saskatchewan, and then only if they work in shops or factories. In 1920 it is extended to include women in hotels and "refreshment rooms" because the government has received complaints about poor pay and long hours. In the House, one Member reports that women receive as little as $4 a week in movie theatres.

The Devolution of Estates Act in Saskatchewan guarantees a widow one-third her husband's estate if she has two or more children, one-half if she has one, and the whole thing if she is childless. (See the Alberta Dower Act of 1911.)

The Saskatchewan Infants Act simply restates the principle of paternal guardianship except for the odd case which has to be decided by the courts.

1920 In Regina, educator Catherine Sheldon-Williams almost single-handedly founds the Outpost Correspondence School for isolated children; in time it will grow into the provincial correspondence school which exists today.

The new *Alberta Infants Act* makes mother and father joint and equal guardians of their children.

The *Saskatchewan Infants Act* is amended to make mothers—not fathers—the usual guardians of children under 14. Fathers are to be guardians of older children. Under new law, if the legal guardian appoints someone else to accept responsibility for a child, the other parent is automatically co-guardian.

1921 Nellie McClung is elected as Liberal member in the Alberta Legislature, a position she will hold until 1926.

Irene Parlby, the first president of the United Farm Women of Alberta, is appointed minister without portfolio in the United Farmers' government. She will stay in office until her retirement in 1935.

Under the Alberta Jury Act women may be called as jurors except in criminal cases but not compelled to serve. A female defendant has a right to women on her jury.

1922 Dr. Frances McGill becomes provincial pathologist for Saskatchewan. A specialist in forensic medicine, she will be named honorary surgeon of the R.C.M.P. in 1946.

Under the *Child Welfare Act* a Manitoba mother gains equal rights to the custody and control of children under 21.

A board with jurisdiction over all urban women wage earners except domestics in private homes is established by The Minimum Wage Act in Alberta. A revised Act will be passed in 1925.

Despite the opposition of Sarah Ramsland, M.L.A., the Saskatchewan government defeats a proposed amendment to the Children's Protection Act which would provide allowances for wives with dependent children if their husbands had not been heard from in five years.

The Married Women's Act in Alberta reaffirms a wife's absolute and unequivocal independence in her own financial and legal dealings.

On February 2, 50 years later, the Women's Press, which will publish this book, is founded.

1923 In Alberta, the Children of Unmarried Parents' Act makes the father responsible for the support of his child.

Zara Nelsova, "Queen of the Cellists", makes her Winnipeg debut in 1915.

1925 Hon. Irene Parlby drafts a Community Property Act which would make anything acquired during a marriage joint property of husband and wife, but it is not passed.

In her award-winning novel, *Wild Geese,* Martha Ostenso takes a cold look at prairie life and a warm look at prairie women.

Violet McNaughton beomes women's editor of *The Western Producer,* she will encourage interest in the mechanization of farm homes, co-operative marketing of eggs and poultry, birth control, married women's property rights, etc.

1926   A national *Ukrainian Women's Association* is organized in Saskatoon, to encourage women to take a leading role in the preservation and advancement of Ukrainian culture on the prairies.

1927   British doctor Dr. Emma Mary Johnstone arrives in Alberta to provide medical care in isolated northern communities. She was instrumental in attracting other women to similar work, e.g. Dr. Mary Percy Jackson who came in 1929 and Dr. Margaret Strang Savage (1931). They took on the work, in Dr. Jackson's words, because "the men had more sense" than to go North. Men with families were tied to settled communities.

1928   On March 14, a petition asking for a ruling on the admission of women to the Canadian Senate reaches the Supreme Court of Canada. It is signed by Emily Murphy, the initiator of the inquiry, and by Nellie McClung, Irene Parlby, Louise McKinney and Henrietta Muir Edwards.

On April 24 the Supreme Court of Canada decides that women are not among the "fit and qualified persons" eligible for the Senate.

Canada's first woman gold medalist, Ethel Catherwood of Saskatoon, wins the women's high jump at the Amsterdam Olympic Games.

1929   On October 18, the Privy Council in London rules that *women are "persons"* qualified to sit in the Senate, thereby overturning a decision of the Supreme Court of Canada.

1930   Canada's first woman Senator, Cairine Wilson of Ontario, is appointed, thanks to the work of Emily Murphy and her friends.

1931   *Prairie population has reached about 2,400,000.*

1936   After a 10-year wait, Lydia Gruchy is ordained by the United Church of Canada at Moose Jaw, Saskatchewan. She is the first—and for many years the only—ordained clergywoman in Canada.

1938   Englishwomen Gweneth Lloyd and Betty Hay-Farally found the Winnipeg Ballet (now the Royal Winnipeg) on a shoestring.

1939   Laura Goodman Salvarson's autobiography *Confessions of an Immigrant's Daughter* is published and wins a Governor-General's Gold Medal.

1940   Mrs. Dorise Nielson from Saskatchewan, is elected to the House of Commons as a United Progressive member. She is the first woman to go to Ottawa from the West. In 1941 she is joined by Cora Casselman of Edmonton. The first woman MP in Canada was Agnes Macphail from Ontario, elected in 1921.

Bibliography

BOOKS AND ARTICLES

A good place to look for information about recent publications on women's history is the *Canadian Newsletter of Research on Women* which is available through the Sociology Department, University of Waterloo, Waterloo, Ontario. Another periodical to watch for is *Atlantis: A Women's Studies Journal* (Box 294, Acadia University, Wolfville, Nova Scotia).

Allan, Gladys L., *Dew Upon the Grass,* Saskatoon, Sask.: Prairie Books, 1963. Memories of a northern Manitoba girlhood beginning in the 1890's. The book describes the way the family struggled to stay alive and the growth of understanding between the white settlers and their Cree neighbours.

Andersen, Margret, *Mother Was Not a Person,* Montreal: Content Publishing Limited and Black Rose Books, 1972. Chapter One, entitled "Woman's Place: How It Was; Examples of Early Canadian Feminism," contains excerpts from the writings of Henrietta Muir Edwards, Nellie McClung and Emily Murphy.

Armitage, May L., "Canada's First Woman Member," *Maclean's,* August 1917, pp. 94-5. A brief biography of Louise McKinney.

——,"Mrs. Nellie McClung," *Maclean's,* July 1915, pp. 37-8.

——, "The First Woman Magistrate in Canada, a character sketch of 'Janey Canuck'," *Maclean's,* October 1916, pp. 27-8.

Atnikov, Pam *et al, Out From the Shadows: A Bibliography of the History of Women in Manitoba,* Manitoba Human Rights Commision, 1975.

Bacchi-Perraro, Carol Lee, *The Ideas of the Canadian Suffragists,* unpublished Master's thesis, McGill, 1969.

Banfill, B.J., *Pioneer Nurse,* Toronto: Ryerson Press, 1967. Autobiography of a woman who worked with pioneers in Saskatchewan during the Depression.

Bannerman, Jean, *Leading Ladies: Canada, 1639 to 1967,* Galt Ont., 1967. One woman's "Who's Who" of Canadian women, past and present. It contains information on dozens of western women.

Bassett, Isabel, *The Parlour Rebellion, Profiles in the Struggle for Women's Rights,* Toronto: McClelland and Stewart, 1975. In addition to chapter-length biographies of Nellie McClung and Emily Murphy, this book makes mention of a few other prairie women such as Louise McKinney and Cora Hind.

Berger, Carl and Cook, Ramsay, ed., *The West and the Nation, Essays in Honour of W.L. Morton,* Toronto: McClelland and Stewart, 1976. Includes and article on Francis Beynon, Winnipeg journalist and suffragist.

Beynon, Francis, *Aleta Dey,* London: 1919. A novel about suffrage, feminism and activism.

Binnie-Clark, Georgina, *A Summer on the Canadian Prairies,* Toronto: Musson Book Co., 1910.

——, *Wheat and Woman,* Toronto: Bell and Cockburn, 1914. Experiences of a British journalist who buys a wheat farm in southern Saskatchewan.

Blackburn, J.H., *Land of Promise,* Toronto: Macmillan of Canada, 1970. One chapter, entitled "A Woman's Work is Never Done", describes the daily work of the author's wife, a farm woman.

Blue, J., *Alberta Past and Present,* Chicago, Illinois: Pioneer Historical Publishing, 1924. A chapter on "Women's Organizations and Activities" briefly describes the development and work of the Alberta branches of the National Council of Women, I.O.D.E., Y.W.C.A., W.C.T.U., V.O.N., Women's Canadian Club, and of the Women's Institutes and United Farm Women.

Bothwell, Jessie Robson, *Pioneers! O Pioneers!,* Regina: Service Printing Co., 1955. A souvenir booklet published for Saskatchewan's "diamond jubilee", it describes pioneer life and achievements; includes biographies of several notable women.

Brigden, Beatrice, "One Woman's Campaign for Social Purity and Social Reform," *The Social Gospel in Canada,* ed. Richard Allen, National Museum of Man, Mercury Series, History Division, Paper No. 9, Ottawa, 1975.

Buck, Ruth Matheson, *The Doctor Rode Side-Saddle,* Toronto: McClelland and Stewart, 1974. The story of Dr. Elizabeth Matheson who began practising medicine at the Onion Lake (Sask.) mission in 1898.

Campbell, Maria, *Halfbreed,* Toronto: McClelland and Stewart, 1973. The moving autobiography of a young Alberta woman.

Campbell, Marjorie W., *The Saskatchewan,* New York: Rinehart, 1950. A chapter on "Free Land, White Women and Wheat" mentions the chores of prairie farm women who lived along the Saskatchewan River.

Caswell, Maryanne, *Pioneer Girl,* Toronto: McGraw-Hill, 1964. The experiences of a child on her way to her family's Saskatchewan homestead.

Cleverdon, Catherine L., *The Woman Suffrage Movement in Canada,* Toronto: University of Toronto Press, 1950, 1974. Though its account of the movement on the prairies is incomplete, this book is still the basic source on the subject.

Colley, Kate, *While Rivers Flow,* Saskatoon, Sask.: Prairie Books, 1970. Autobiography of a district nurse in the early days of settlement.

Cormack, Barbara Villy, *Perennials and Politics, the Life Story of Hon. Irene Parlby,* Sherwood Park, Alberta, 1968.

——, *The Red Cross Lady,* Edmonton, Alberta: The Institute of Applied Arts, 1960. A biography of Mary H. Conquest.

Corrective Collective, *Never Done: Three Centuries of Women's Work in Canada,* Toronto: Canadian Women's Educational Press, 1974. An attractive, warm, witty, delightfully illustrated look at the work of ordinary Canadian women.

——, *She Named It Canada Because That's What It Was Called,* Toronto: Canadian Women's Educational Press (4th edition), 1975.

Crawford, Mary Elizabeth, *Legal Status of Women in Manitoba as Shown by Extracts from Dominion and Provincial Laws.* Manitoba Political Equality League, 1913.

Davis, Mrs. Mary, "A Pinafored Printer," *Saskatchewan History,* Spring 1956, pp. 63-9. Mrs. Davis worked in the office of the *Regina Leader* between 1886 and 1890.

Duncan, Joy, *Red Serge Wives,* Edmonton: Centennial Book Committee, 1974. Women with the Royal North West Mounted Police.

Gibbon, John M. and Mathewson, Mary, *Three Centuries of Canadian Nursing,* Toronto: Macmillan, 1947. Includes a brief chapter on the development of nursing service and hospitals in each of the prairie provinces.

Gray, James H., *Red Lights on the Prairies,* Toronto: Macmillan, 1971. A study of prostitution on the prairies from 1900 to 1925. Not much information on the women themselves.

Hacker, Carlotta, *The Indomitable Lady Doctors,* Toronto: Clarke Irwin, 1974. A well-researched book which chronicles the efforts of women to break into an all-male field. The prairie doctors discussed are Charlotte Ross, Amelia Yeomans, Elizabeth Scott Matheson, Mary Crawford, Mary Percy Jackson, Evelyn Windsor, Rosamond Leacock.

Haig, Kennethe, *Brave Harvest: the Life Story of E. Cora Hind, L.L.D.,* Toronto: Thomas Allen, 1945. Little information on her work in the W.C.T.U. or the suffrage movement.

Hall, Margaret Ann, *A History of Women's Sport in Canada Prior to World War I,* unpublished Master's thesis, University of Alberta.

Hall, Mary Georgina, *A Lady's Life on a Farm in Manitoba,* London: W.H.Allen and Co., 1884.

Healey, W.J., *Women of Red River,* Winnipeg, Manitoba: Peguis Publishers, 1923. The stories of the first white women to come west, written from their recollections. Covers the period from 1806 to 1879.

Hiemstra, Mary, *Gully Farm,* Toronto: McClelland and Stewart, 1955. The story of the Barr colonists by a woman who made the trek as a child.

Holmes, Mrs. Robert, "Experiences of a Missionary's Wife," *Alberta Historical Review,* Spring 1964, pp. 18-25.

Inderwick, Mary E., "A Lady and her Ranche," *Alberta Historical Review,* Autumn 1967, pp. 1-9. This entire edition is about pioneer women.

Innis, Mary Quayle, *The Clear Spirit: Twenty Canadian Women and Their Times,* Toronto: University of Toronto Press, 1967. Includes a chapter on the Person's Case.

Jackson, Dr. Mary Percy, *On the Last Frontier: Pioneering in the Peace River Block,* Toronto, 1933. The letters of a frontier doctor to her family in England.

Jameson, Sheilagh J., "Give Your Other Vote to the Sister," *Alberta Historical Review,* Autumn 1967, pp. 10-16. A biography of Roberta MacAdams.

Johnston, Jean, *Wilderness Women,* Toronto: Peter Martin Associates, 1973. Biographies of women who "planted the roots of settlement in the New World," i.e. Canada, including the first white woman known to have resided in the West, Marie-Anne Lagimodière.

Kaye, V.J., *Early Ukrainian Settlements in Canada 1895-1900,* Toronto: University of Toronto Press, 1964.

Kells, Edna, *Elizabeth McDougall,* Toronto: United Church Publishing House. A pamphlet, the biography of the wife and mother of a frontier Protestant missionary family.

Lindal, Walter (Vladimar) Jacobson, *The Saskatchewan Icelanders,* Winnipeg: Columbia Press, 1955.

Lloyd, Wynham Edward Buckley, *One Hundred Years of Medicine,* London: Duckworth, 1936. Includes information on women in medicine on the prairies.

Mahood, Sally, "The Women's Suffrage Movement in Canada and Saskatchewan," *Women Unite!* Toronto: Canadian Women's Educational Press, 1972, pp. 21-30. The author argues that Saskatchewan feminists achieved a more profound analysis of women's place in society than did suffragists elsewhere in Canada.

Matheson, Gwen, ed., *Women in the Canadian Mosaic,* Toronto: Peter Martin Associates, 1975. Includes articles on Nellie McClung and the suffrage movement.

McClung, Nellie, *Clearing in the West,* Toronto: Thomas Allen, 1935, 1964. Volume I of her autobiography, from her birth to her marriage.

——, *In Times Like These,* Toronto: McLeod and Allen, 1915; University of Toronto Press, 1972. Essays on feminism and pacifism. The introduction to the 1972 edition describes Mrs. McClung's life and work.

——, *The Stream Runs Fast,* Toronto: Thomas Allen, 1945, 1965. Volume II of her autobiography.

MacDonald, Christine, "How Saskatchewan Women Got the Vote," *Saskatchewan History,* I, No. 3, 1948, pp. 1-8.

McDougall, Mrs. John, "Incidents of Mission Life, 1874," *Alberta Historical Review,* Winter 1966, pp.26-39.

McKinlay, Clare M., "The Honorable Irene Parlby," unpublished Master's thesis, University of Alberta, 1953.

MacLean, Una, "The Honorable Irene Parlby," *Alberta Historical Review,* Spring 1959, pp. 1-6.

——, "The Famous Five," *Alberta Historical Review,* Spring 1952, pp.1-4. The Persons Case.

Menzies, June, "Votes for Saskatchewan Women," *Politics in Saskatchewan,* ed. N.Ward and D. Spafford, Don Mills, Ontario: Longman's 1968, pp. 78-92. An interestingly written account of the key women and organizations; a good analysis of the inter-relationship between issues, particularly temperance and suffrage.

Murphy, Emily, *Janey Canuck in the West,* Cassell and Co., 1910; J.M.Dent and Sons, 1917.

——, *Open Trails,* Cassell and Co., 1912; J.M.Dent and Sons, 1920.

——, *Seeds of Pine,* Hodder and Stoughton, 1914; Musson Book Co., 1922. All three books are accounts of her experiences and travels in western Canada.

——, "What Janey Thinks of Nellie," *Maclean's,* September 1, 1921, pp. 15, 34-5. An affectionate look at Nellie McClung at the time of her election to the Alberta Legislature.

National Council of Women of Canada, *Women of Canada, Their Life and Work,* prepared for distribution at the Glasgow International Exhibition, 1901. A very thorough handbook on the history, achievements and position of Canadian women, including discussions of their legal and political status, their organizations, and their work in trade, industry, professions, the arts, the church, charities and social reform.

Nicholson, B.J., *Feminism in Western Canada to 1916,* unpublished Master's thesis, University of Calgary, 1972.

Ostenso, Martha, *Wild Geese,* New York: Dodd, Mead, 1925; Toronto: McClelland and Stewart, 1961. A novel centering on the conflict between a Northern Manitoba pioneer and his stormy daughter.

Parsons, Nell, *Upon a Sagebrush Harp,* Saskatoon: Sask. Prairie Books, 1969. A girl's account of an unsuccessful attempt to homestead.

Rendell, Alice, "Letters from a Barr Colonist," *Alberta Historical Review,* Winter 1963, pp. 12-27. Mrs. Rendell was an upper class British woman.

Roberts, Sarah Ellen, *Of Us and Oxen,* Saskatoon: Sask. Prairie Books, 1968. Homesteading in Alberta.

Roe, Amy J., "Canada's Woman Cabinet Minister," *Maclean's,* June 15, 1925, pp. 94, 98. Irene Parlby.

Salverson, Laura Goodman, *Confessions of an Immigrant's Daughter,* Toronto: McClelland, 1939. An autobiography; Icelandic settlement in Manitoba.

Sanders, Byrne Hope, *Emily Murphy, Crusader,* Toronto: Macmillan, 1945.

——, *Famous Women: Carr, Hind, Gullen, Murphy,* Toronto: Clarke Irwin, 1958. Brief biographies of Emily Carr, E. Cora Hind, Augusta Stowe Gullen and Emily Murphy.

Savage, Candace, *Foremothers: Personalities and Issues from the History of Women in Saskatchewan,* available from the author at 350 Carleton Drive, Saskatoon, Saskatchewan.

Saskatoon Women's Calendar Collective, *Herstory: A Canadian Women's Calendar, 1974* and *1975,* Toronto: Canadian Women's Educational Press, 1973, 1974; *Herstory 1976* and *1977,* Edmonton: Hurtig, 1975 and 1976. A calendar noting historical and contemporary Canadian women.

Schaeffer, Mary T.S., *Old Indian Trails of the Canadian Rockies,* Toronto: William Briggs, 1911. Tells of her official "discovery" of Maligne Lake in Jasper National Park.

Shaw, Rosa, *Proud Heritage,* Toronto: Ryerson Press, 1957. A History of the National Council of Women in Canada.

Some Saskatchewan Legislation Affecting Women and Children, Regina: King's Printers, 1921.

Strange, K., *With the West in Her Eyes,* New York: Dodge, 1937. The experiences of a woman on a Western Canadian farm in the 1920s.

Strong-Boag, Veronica, "Cousin Cinderella," *Women in Canada,* ed. Marylee Stephenson, Toronto: New Press, 1973, pp. 291-326. A bibliography of material on women's history in Canada.

Sykes, Ella C., *A Home-Help in Canada,* London: Smith, Elder, 1915. In order to gather practical information, an English writer travelled across Canada as a domestic, working for six months in five different Canadian homes. An excellent description of the work and living conditions of women immigrating to Western Canada as either servants or wives.

Thomson, Georgina H., *Crocus and Meadowlark Country,* Edmonton: Institute of Applied Arts, 1963.

Van Kirk, Sylvia, "Thanadelthur," *The Beaver,* Spring 1974, pp. 40-45. The story of a Chipewyan woman who worked as an agent of the Hudson's Bay Company in th early 1700s.

——, "Women and the Fur Trade," *The Beaver,* Winter 1972, pp. 4-21.

Voisey, Paul, "The 'Votes for Women' Movement," *Alberta History,* Summer 1975, pp. 1-23.

Wright, J.F.C., *The Louise Lucas Story: This Time Tomorrow,* Montreal: Harvest House, 1965. Biography of the woman described as "Mother of the Saskatchewan C.C.F."

Wright, Myrtle Hayes, "Mothering the Prairie," *Maclean's,* April 1, 1926, pp. 22,83. Violet McNaughton.

Youmans, Letitia, *Campaign Echoes,* Toronto: William Briggs, 1898. Autobiography of the founder of the Canadian W.C.T.U.

FILMS

The Visible Woman. Half-hour colour documentary on the struggle for women's rights in Canada. Distributed by the Federation of Women Teachers Associations of Ontario, 1260 Bay St., Toronto, Ontario.

Great Grand Mother. Half-hour colour documentary on the role played by women in the settlement of the Canadian prairies. Available at any National Film Board distribution office.

The Grain of Truth. Both a slide-tape presentation and a 15 minute black and white film, on the issue of property rights based on cartoons published in the 1914 *Grain Growers' Guide.* Distributed by Magpie Media, No. 4—10805 124th St., Edmonton, Alberta.

A NOTE ON ARCHIVE COLLECTIONS

Much of the material in this book is drawn from archive collections. The accounts of *Saskatchewan Homesteading Experiences* are in the Public Archives of Canada. Transcripts of letters written by Louisa Jame, Amey McDougall and material on the United Farm Women of Alberta are held by the Provincial Archives of Alberta. The papers of Nellie McClung and Emily Murphy are in the archives of British Columbia and of Edmonton, respectively. A few of Irene Parlby's papers are available from the Glenbow-Alberta Institute in Calgary, which also holds the letters of Mrs. Rendell, "A Lady's Life on the Ranch" by Mrs. Charles Inderwick, "A Start for the Great West" by Mrs. John Willis and *Across Canada's Pioneer Trails* by Margaret Lawrence. The Saskatchewan Archives in Saskatoon hold the papers of Violet McNaughton, Premier Walter Scott, Mrs. S. N. Haight, the Women Grain Growers' Association and the United Farmers of Canada (Saskatchewan Section). The Regina office has the papers of the Saskatchewan W.C.T.U. The records of the Manitoba W.C.T.U. are at the Provincial Archives of Manitoba, along with papers of the Manitoba Political Equality League, the Canadian Women's Press Club, the Manitoba Equal Suffrage Club and information on Lillian Beynon Thomas. The Manitoba Archives also holds transcripts of an interview with Mrs. Stidson, the "Story of a Cruel Father" by Lizzie Johnson, "Against the Wind" by Lucie Johnson, and *Pioneer Prairie Profiles* by Laura Vivian Belvadere (Todd) Arnett. The Manitoba Provincial Library has an extensive collection of prairie newspapers.

Credits

BOOKS

Allen, Gladys, *Dew Upon the Grass,* Prairie Books, Saskatoon, 1963; Davis, Mary, "A Pinafored Printer", *Saskatchewan History,* 1956, vol. 14; Ferguson, Emily, *Janey Canuck in the West,* J.M. Dent, Toronto, 1917; Leonoff, Cyril Edel, *Wapella Farm Settlement: A Pictorial History,* the Jewish Historical Society of Western Canada Inc., and the Manitoba Historical Society, Winnipeg; McClung, Nellie, *Clearing in the West and The Stream Runs Fast,* Thomas Allen, Toronto, 1935, 1964 and 1945, 1965; McClung, Nellie, *In Times Like These,* University of Toronto Press, Toronto, 1972, pp. 44-45, 91; "Mrs. Hoffman's Story", *Pioneer Tales of the Interlake,* Interlake Publishing Ltd., Stonewall, Manitoba; Roberts, Sarah Ellen, *Of Us and Oxen,* Prairie Books, Saskatoon, 1968; Sanders, Byrne Hope, *Emily Murphy, Crusader,* Macmillan of Canada Ltd., 1945; *Leaves from the Medicine Tree,* High River Historical Society.

PHOTOGRAPHS

Canadian Pacific
11

Glenbow-Alberta Institute
15, 29, 31, 41, 45, 47, 53, 59, 67, 77, 85, 87, 93, 99, 103, 107, 109, 111, 121, 125, 131, 135, 141, 143, 151, 155, 165, 169, 171, 173, 189, 199, 203, 211, 215, 221
Dr. Simpson Photo Collection: 37

Provincial Archives of Alberta
63, 65, 205
E. Brown Collection: 33, 35, 61, 73, 79, 219

Provincial Archives of Manitoba
19, 51, 83, 101, 115, 137, 139, 153, 163, 167, 179, 191, 207

Provincial Archives of Saskatchewan
201

Public Archives of Canada
17(C52819); 21(C9652); 23(C4745); 25(PA10270); 39(C16926); 57(PA19134); 71(C30937); 75(C30784); 81(C30938); 105(PA13284); 113(C18734); 119(C30948); 133(C45390); 183(C8482); 217(C29974)

Provincial Archives of Victoria
185, 197

Saskatoon Public Library 183(C8482); 217(C29974)
27

Index